CROCHET

CROCHET

EBURY PRESS
LONDON

Chief Contributor/
Project Editor
Dorothea Hall

Art Editor
Michele Walker

Editor
Miren Lopategui

Designer
Sue Rawkins

Assistant
Lesley Prescott

Managing Editor
Amy Carroll

Managing Art Editor
Debbie Mackinnon

Crochet
was conceived, edited and designed by Dorling Kindersley Limited,
9 Henrietta Street, London WC2E 8PS

First published in Great Britain in 1981 by
Ebury Press,
an imprint of the Random Century Group
Random Century House
20 Vauxhall Bridge Road
London SW1V 2SA

Reprinted in 1990

ISBN 0 85223 955 6

Printed in Singapore

Contents

Introduction

Crochet is an immensely satisfying craft. It is simple and quick to work and, like knitting, is practical and portable and has become an extremely popular pastime. Throughout history crochet has been closely associated with knitting, so much so that it was not surprising that, with the introduction of many machine-washable knitting yarns, an interest in all forms of crochet was also revived.

Today, there are many specially-produced crochet yarns available ranging from the very finest cotton – in plain and random-dyed colours, shimmery lurex and glistening bead-like threads – to thick chunky yarns.

The origins of crochet-stitch patterns are obscure but crochet and other wool crafts have been practised in the Middle East for thousands of years. Over the Renaissance period crochet patterns developed in imitation of Guipure and Richelieu laces and needlepoint embroidery, introducing, for example, single motifs tied with picot bars. This technique was fully developed by crochet workers in Ireland – from Cork in the south to Monaghan in the north. The Irish introduced to their crochet rural motifs such as farmyard animals, the wheel, rose and shamrock.

Some time later it was discovered that crochet could be worked into a complete fabric and not be restricted to lacy edgings and insertions.

Stitch patterns in this book include flat, ridged and raised fabric stitches, textured puffball and loop stitches, with information for working traditional Irish net patterns, Tunisian crochet and edgings, and many more, with present-day techniques for working medallions and colourwork patterns.

The aim throughout is to guide the crocheter through all the techniques and to give a new dimension to the ways in which these crochet stitch patterns can be applied and extended.

All you need to begin to explore the myriad possibilities of crochet are a hook and yarn. With these the door is open to making many beautiful things for your family and home.

BASIC TECHNIQUE

HOOKS
Crochet hooks are machine-made, usually from plastic-coated aluminium or steel. They are made in a range of sizes, conforming to the International Standard Range (ISR), from 0.60, for fine cottons, to 10.00, for working very thick rug yarn. Since the hooks do not hold stitches but hold only the working loop, they are all made to a standard length. Tunisian crochet hooks are also available in metric sizes but are made in varying lengths to accommodate the correct number of stitches required.

WHICH YARN?
Choose the most appropriate yarn, hook and stitch pattern to suit your special needs. Generally, very fine yarns and hooks are used for delicate lacy effects, medium-weights for more practical fabrics, heavy-weights for warmth and hard-wearing qualities.

YARNS
In addition to a very wide range of specially-produced crochet threads, most yarns that are manufactured for knitting, knotting and weaving can be used.

Yarn describes any thread spun from natural fibres such as wool, cotton, linen, silk, or synthetics.

Ply indicates the number of spun single threads which have been twisted together to produce a specific yarn. Single threads may be spun to any thickness so that ply does not refer to a standard thickness of yarn, although the terms 2-, 3- and 4-ply are often used to describe yarns of a recognized thickness. For instance, we might say that a particular spinner's yarn will "knit-up" to a 4-ply weight.

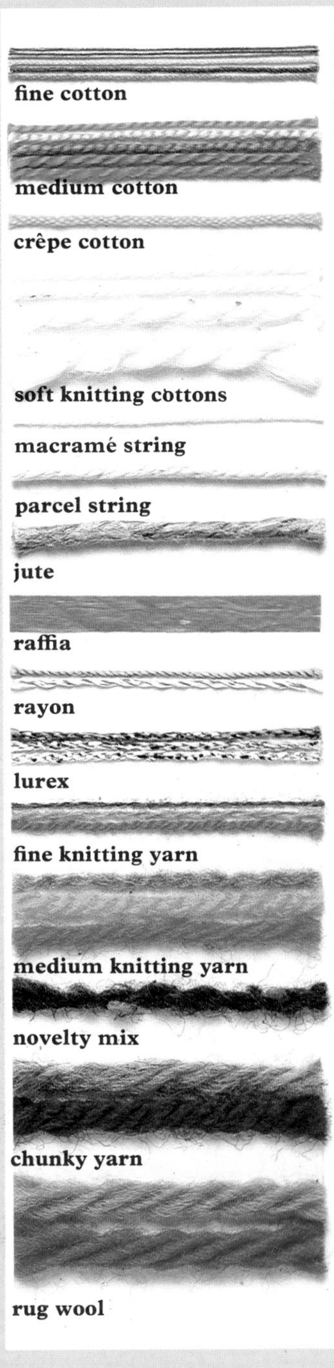

THE FOUNDATION CHAIN

To begin crochet, a slip loop is placed on the hook. This is a working loop and is never counted as a stitch. Stitches are made by pulling one loop through another to form a foundation chain upon which the next row or round is worked.

CHAIN STITCH (ch)

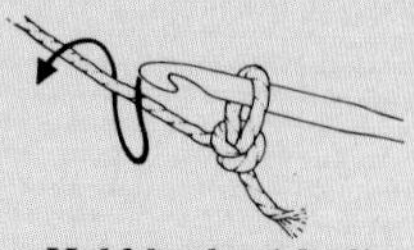

1 *Hold back with slip loop in RH, twist hook under and over yarn.*

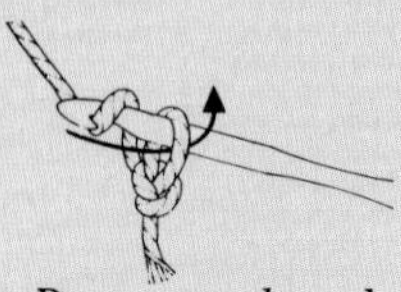

2 *Draw yarn through slip loop on hook.*

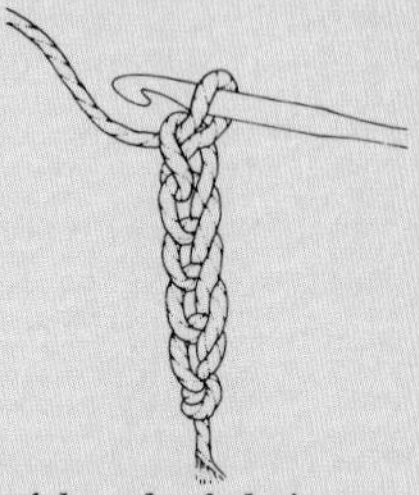

A length of chain sts.

DOUBLE CHAIN STITCH (dch)

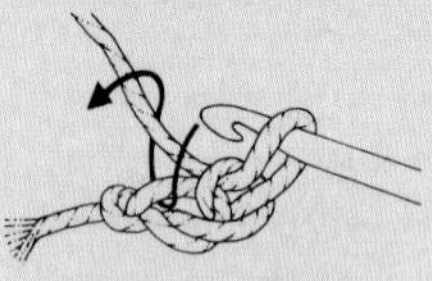

1 *Make slip loop and work 2 ch, insert hook into 1st ch, yarn round hook (yrh), draw loop through.*

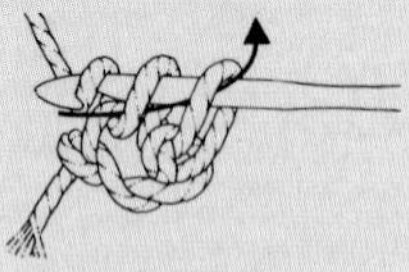

2 *Yarn round hook, draw through both loops on hook. Repeat steps 1 and 2.*

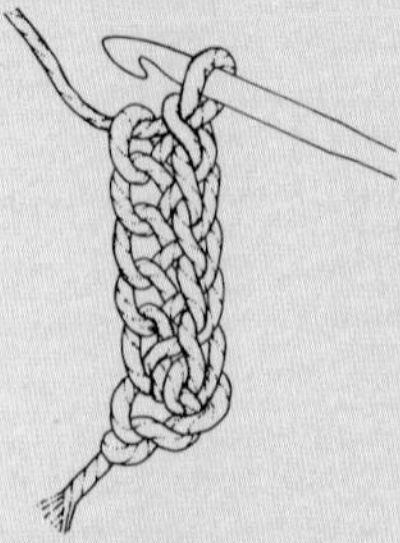

Use dchs for firm edge.

FINISHING OFF

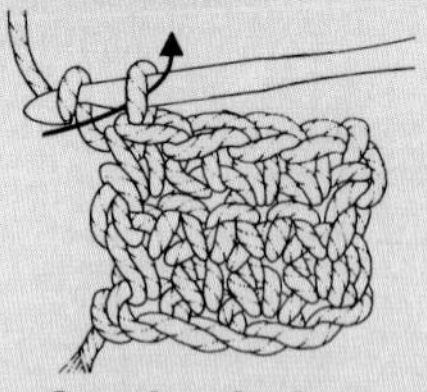

1 *Complete final st and cut yarn about 15 cm from work. Pull through last loop and tighten.*

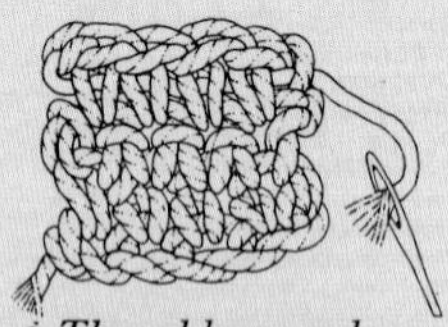

2 *Thread loose end into yarn needle and darn into back of work.*

COUNTING

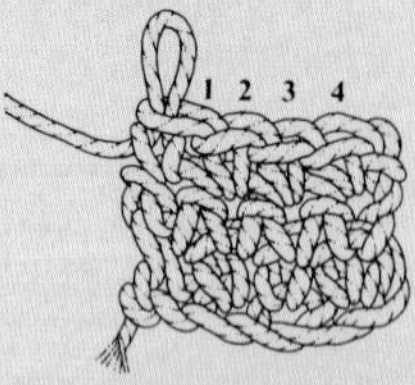

Count dc as above. In trebles count 1 upright as 1 st. Count 1 ch between 2 tr as 3 sts.

TURNING CHAINS (t-ch)

Extra chains are worked at the end of a row before turning to bring the hook to the correct depth of the stitch being worked, so that the first stitch can be made evenly.

Table giving number of turning chains required for each stitch

double crochet:	1 turning chain
half treble:	2 turning chains
treble:	3 turning chains
double treble:	4 turning chains
triple treble:	5 turning chains

BASIC STITCHES

Each stitch gives a different texture and varies in depth, and every row makes a new chain line into which the next row is worked. Where stitches are worked back and forth in rows there is no right or wrong side to the fabric. *Note:* turning chain (**t-ch**) forms first stitch in row.

SINGLE CROCHET/SLIP STITCH (ss)

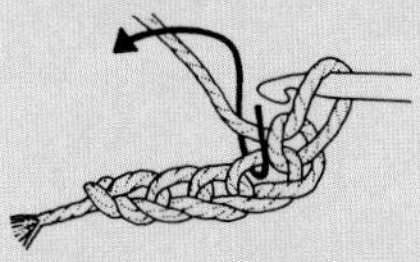

1 *Make no. of ch. Insert hook from F to B into 2nd ch from hook.*

2 *Yrh, draw through 2 loops on hook. Repeat steps 1 and 2 to end.*

3 *Make 1 t-ch, turn, insert hook into B of first st of last row.*

DOUBLE CROCHET (dc)

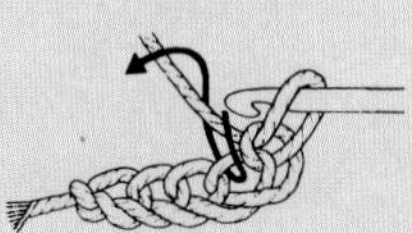

1 *Make ch row. Insert hook into 2nd ch from hook, yrh, draw through.*

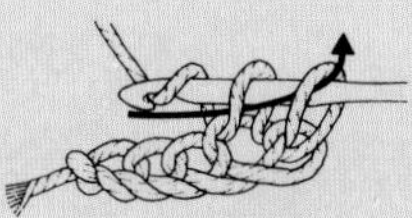

2 *Yrh, draw through 2 loops. Repeat steps 1 and 2 to end.*

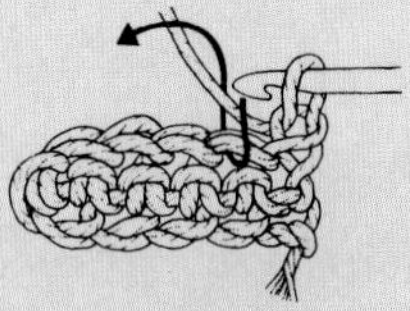

3 *1 t-ch, turn, insert hook under both loops of 1st st of last row.*

HALF TREBLE (htr)

1 *Make ch row. Yrh and insert into 3rd ch, yrh, draw through.*

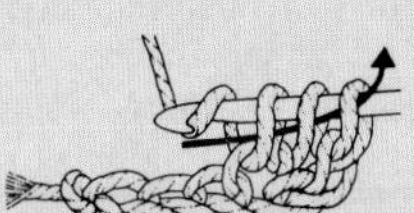

2 *Yrh, draw through 3 loops. Cont working htr into every ch to end.*

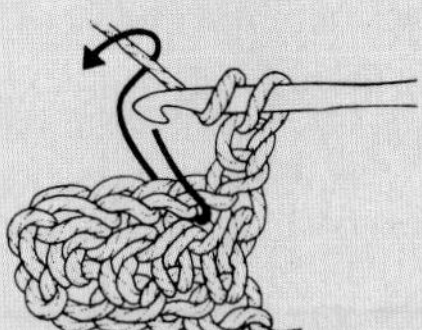

3 *2 t-chs, turn. Make 1 htr into 1st st of last row, rep to end.*

TREBLE (tr)

1 *Make ch row. Yrh, insert into 5th ch, yrh, draw 1 loop through.*

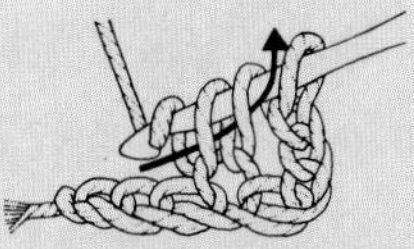

2 *Yrh, draw through first 2 lps on hook, rep one more.*

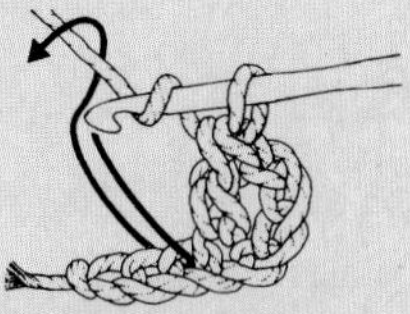

3 *Cont to end, 3 t-ch, turn. Make 1 tr into 2nd st of last row.*

DOUBLE TREBLE (dtr)

1 *Make ch row. Yrh twice, insert into 6th ch from hook, yrh, draw lp through.*

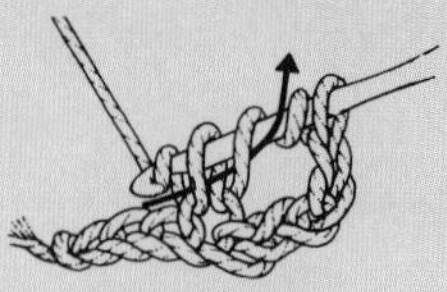

2 *Yrh and draw through first 2 lps on hook. Rep step 2 twice more.*

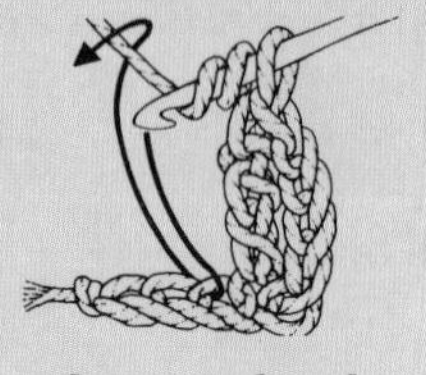

3 *Cont to end, make 4 t-ch, turn. Make first dtr into 2nd st of row below.*

TRIPLE TREBLE (tr tr)

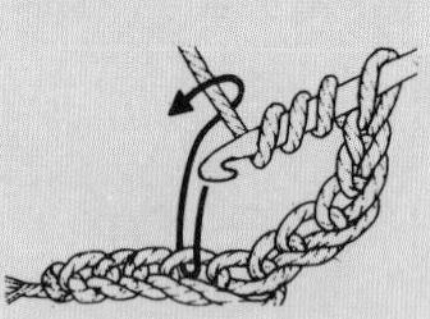

1 *Make ch row. Yrh 3 times, insert into 7th ch from hook, yrh, draw loop through.*

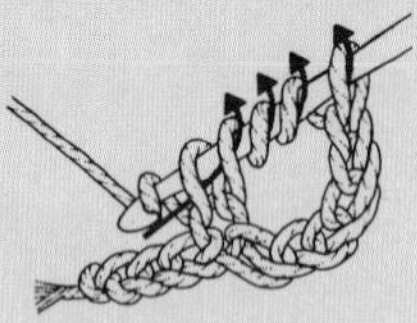

2 *Yrh and draw through first 2 lps on hook. Rep this step 3 times more.*

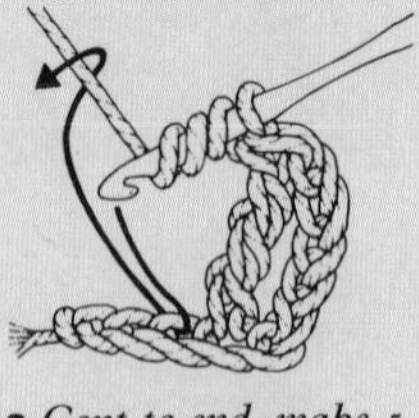

3 *Cont to end, make 5 t-ch, turn. Make first tr tr into 2nd st of row below.*

SEAMS AND EDGES

Crochet sections may be joined together by sewing, using a blunt-ended wool needle with matching yarn, and a back stitch or woven seam as appropriate. You can also use double crochet; this gives a very firm seam and is often worked as an edging in a contrasting colour on the right side of the fabric. Make sure that patterns such as stripes, shells or clusters match exactly before sewing.

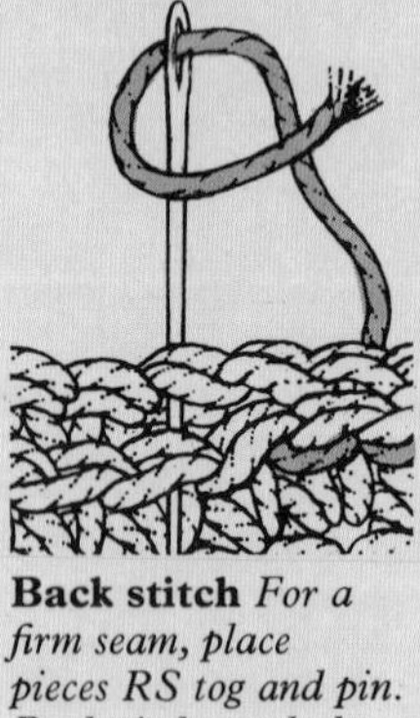

Back stitch *For a firm seam, place pieces RS tog and pin. Backstitch evenly between crochet stitches.*

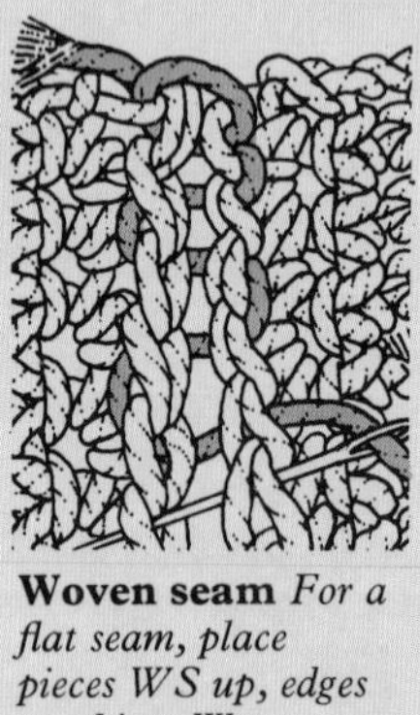

Woven seam *For a flat seam, place pieces WS up, edges touching. Weave needle loosely around both edge sts.*

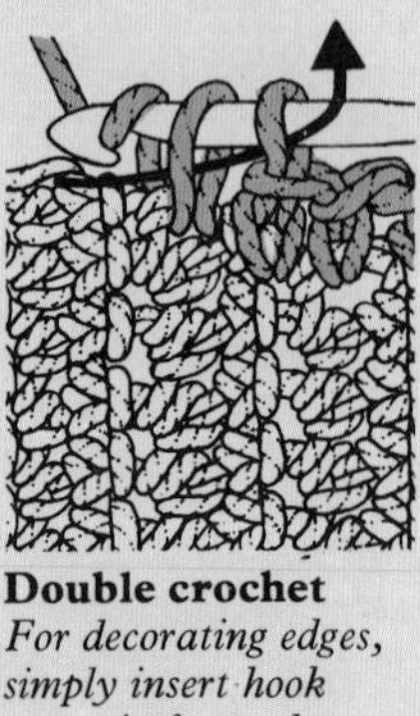

Double crochet *For decorating edges, simply insert hook one st in from edge, work dc evenly through sts.*

BASIC STITCH VARIATIONS

Interesting variations to the basic stitches are made by inserting the hook into different parts of the stitch below and twisting the yarn in different ways.

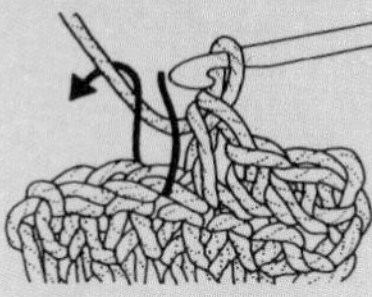

Crossed double crochet
Work as for dc but take hook over *yarn and draw loop through.*

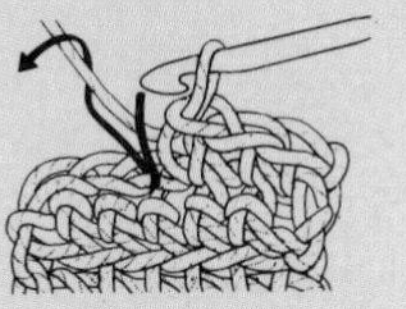

Working into half of stitch below
For RS ridge, insert hook into back of st in row below; into front of st for WS ridge.

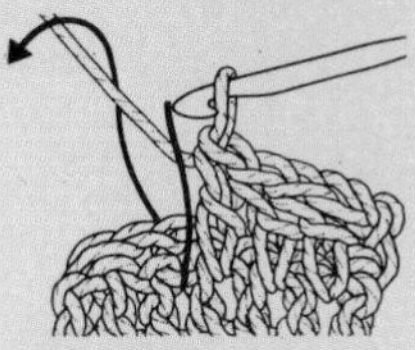

Working between stitches
Insert hook into space between 2 sts in row below.

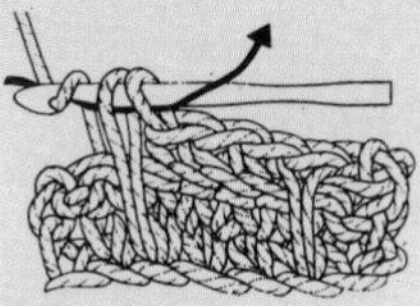

Working into stitches 2 rows below
Insert hook front to back between 2 sts, 2 rows below.

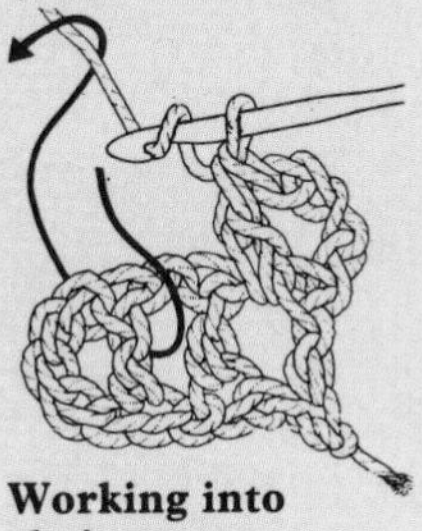

Working into chain space
Insert hook into space between ch sts in row below.

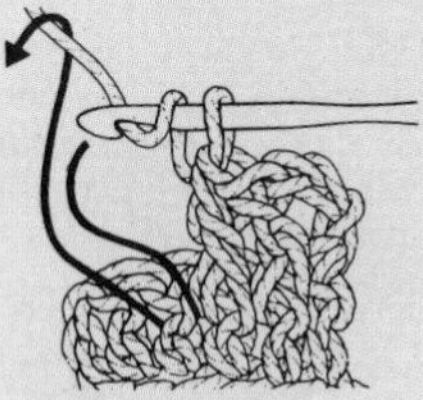

Working a raised effect
Insert hook from front around st below. For indented effect, insert hook from back.

TEXTURED STITCHES

Textures are created by working into the same stitch several times, as in bobble patterns, or by wrapping the yarn around the hook several times before drawing through, as in bullion stitch.

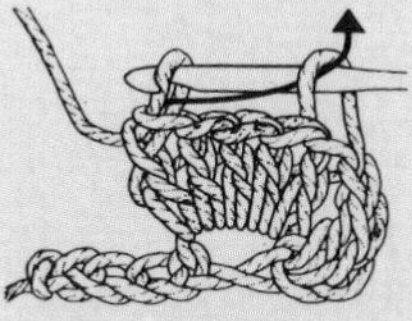

Bobble stitch
5 tr into next st, withdraw hook, insert into 1st tr, pick up lp, draw through.

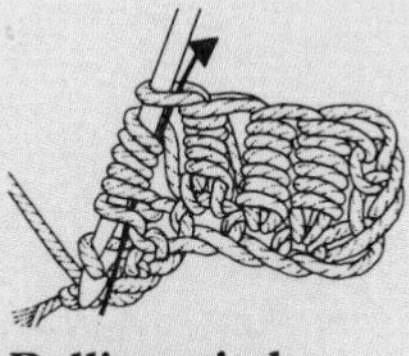

Bullion stitch
Yrh several times, insert hook into ch, yrh, draw through, yrh, draw through all loops.

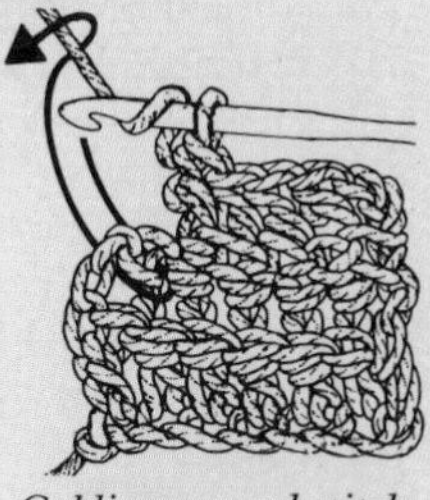

Cabling around stitch.

Yrh, insert hook from back to front around tr in row below, work 1 tr.

LOOP STITCH

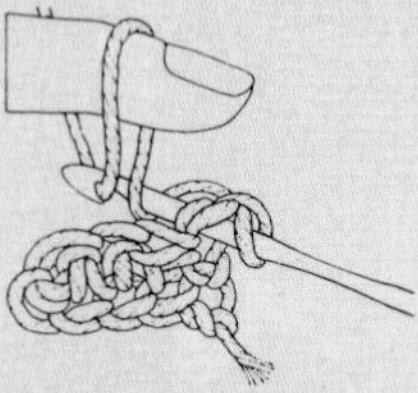

1 *Wrap yarn around L forefinger, insert hook into first st, catch both strands.*

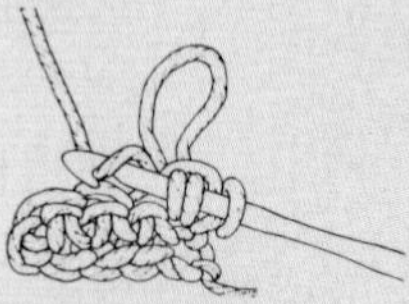

2 *Draw 2 lps through drop lp from finger, yrh. Draw through 3 lps on hook.*

3 *Rep steps 1 and 2 to end. Work 1 row dc before next lp row.*

OPENWORK STITCHES

Openwork mesh patterns are formed by missing stitches and working chains over the spaces left; the simplest way to make lacy crochet. Various patterns can be made by altering the combination of stitches and spaces.

Simple openwork

Work 1 tr, 2ch, miss 2 ch in previous row, 1 tr into next ch. Rep to end.

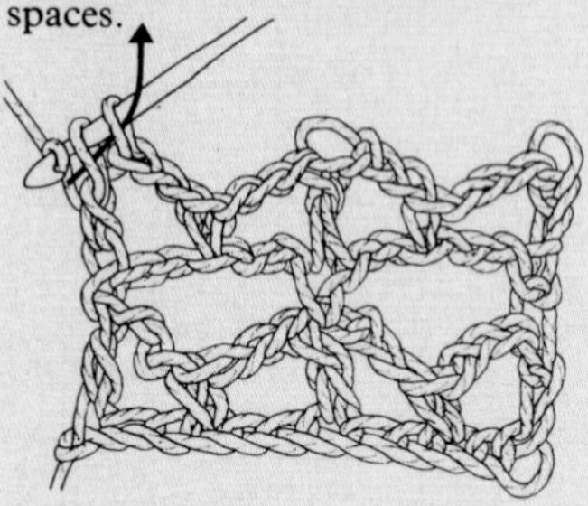

Bar and lattice

1 tr, 3 ch, miss 2 ch in row below, 1 dc into next ch, 3 ch, miss 2 ch. Rep to end.

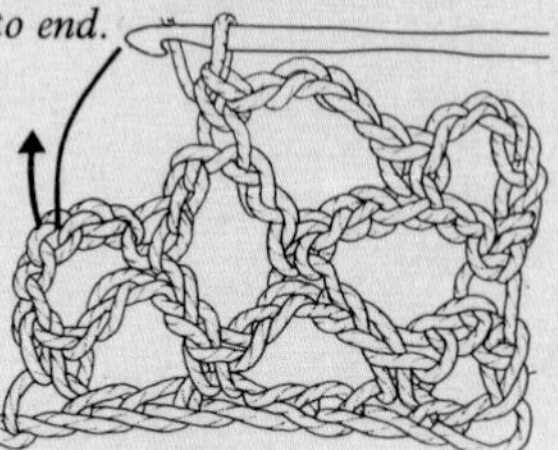

Simple net ground

Work 1 dc into 5th ch of row below, 5 ch, rep to end.

ADDING NEW YARN

Use these methods for joining in a new yarn or colour. In small colour patterns yarn not in use is carried along top of row below until required. Vertical or diagonal stripes require a ball of yarn for each colour; twist once as new colour is picked up.

New yarn in dc

1 *Run new yarn along top of previous row, work over it as if part of row below. When needed introduce with last yrh of dc.*

2 *If old yarn is reqd again in row carry along as step 1. If not, cut off after few sts. Leave at back if reqd in same place next row.*

NEW YARN IN TR

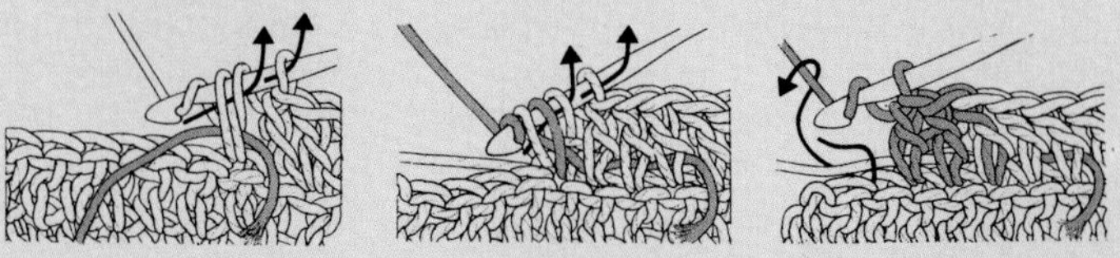

1 *Carry new yarn along top of previous row until required. Yrh with old yarn, insert hook.*

2 *Yrh with both yarns, draw through. Yrh with new yarn and complete tr.*

3 *Carry old yarn along top of previous row until reqd. If not, cut off after a few sts.*

WORKING IN THE ROUND

Circular crochet is worked continuously around a central point starting with a foundation ring. The crochet can either be worked as a flat medallion, shaped as a beret or as a tube. Where a small number of chains are required use a ring of single crochet, joined with a slip stitch. Where a large number of chains are required use a ring of double crochet.

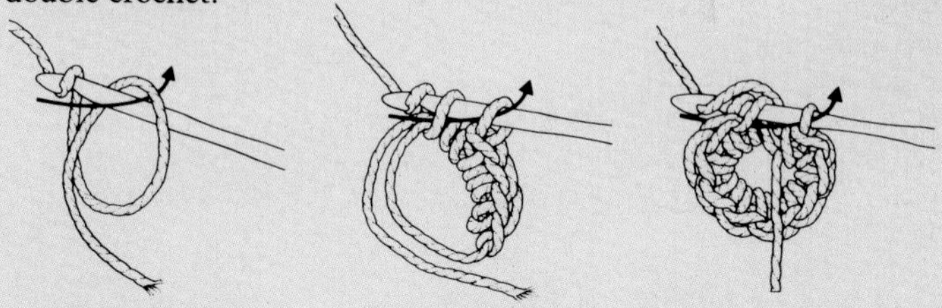

1 *Make a circle with yarn as shown. Insert hook, yrh, draw through circle, yrh, draw through loop.*

2 *Work required number of dc around circle and over both strands.*

3 *Pull loose end firmly to draw circle together. Close ring with a slip stitch.*

TUNISIAN CROCHET

Tunisian crochet is worked with a number of stitches carried on a single hook. The stitches are worked from a foundation row of chains. Stitches for the first row are picked up working from right to left. Then, on the second row, working from left to right, stitches are made and discarded without turning the work around.

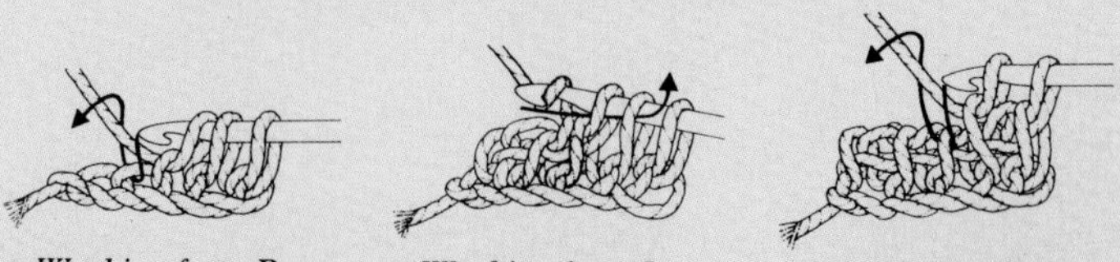

1 *Working from R to L, insert hook into ch, yrh, draw lp through. Cont to end.*

2 *Working from L to R, yrh, draw through 1st lp, *yrh, draw through 2 lps, rep from * to end.*

3 *For all R to L rows, insert hook through vertical lp of st below. Rep steps 1 and 2.*

INCREASING (inc)

Crochet will become wider by increasing the number of stitches in a row or round. The simplest method is to work extra stitches into the same stitch either at the beginning, at both ends, or in the middle of a row, as a single or double increase.

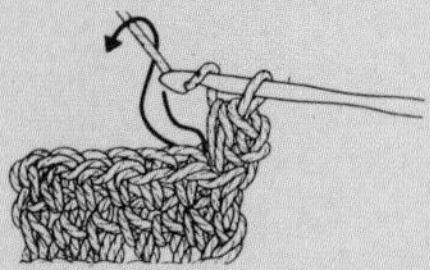

Single increase at each end of row
Work twice into first or last st.

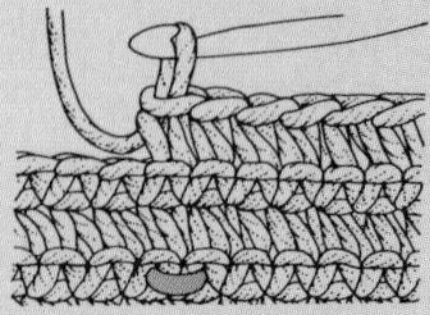

Single increase in middle of row
Work twice into any st. Mark st with contrast yarn.

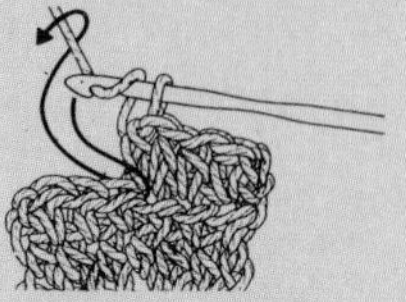

Double increases
Work 3 times into same st on previous row.

MULTIPLE INCREASES

Several stitches may be increased at the edge of the work by making extra chain stitches.

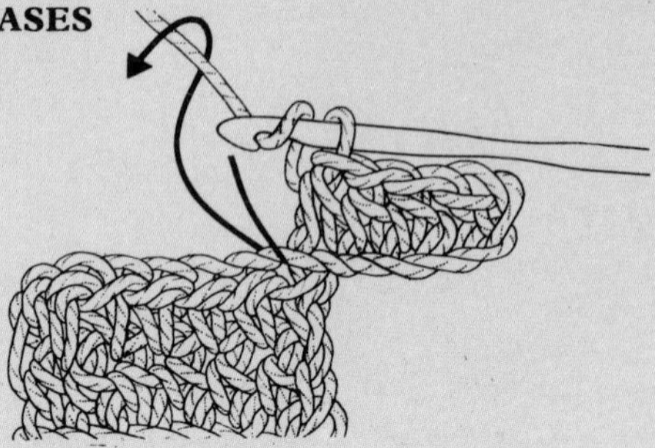

Adding stitches at beginning of row
Make same no. of extra ch as sts reqd plus t-chs, turn. Work new sts in pattern.

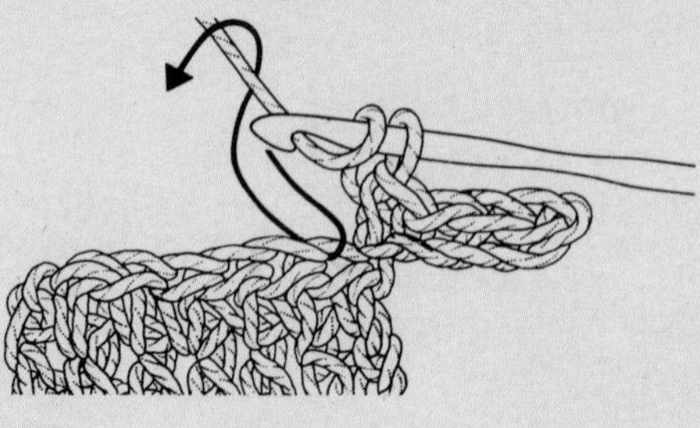

Adding stitches at end of row
To keep increases made at both ends of row level make provision for these stitches on previous row.
1 *Make same no. of extra ch as sts reqd plus t-chs. Work ss over new ch, cont in pattern.*

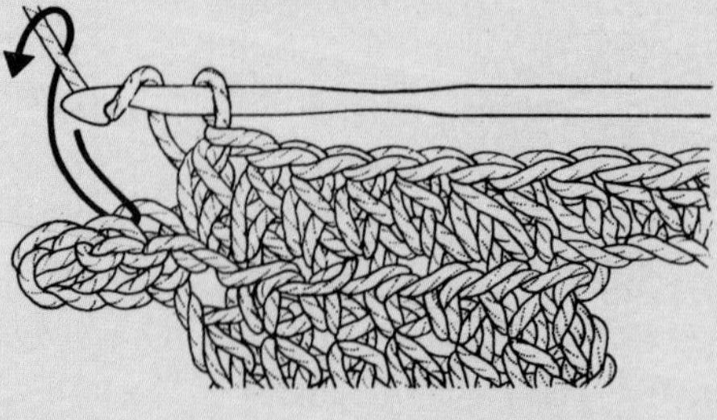

2 *On next row, continue to end in pattern working through slip stitches.*

DECREASING (dec)

Crochet will become narrower by decreasing the number of stitches in a row. The simplest method is to miss a stitch either at the beginning, the middle or the end of a row. Alternative methods are; to decrease at the edge by leaving stitches unworked or to work two stitches together as one.

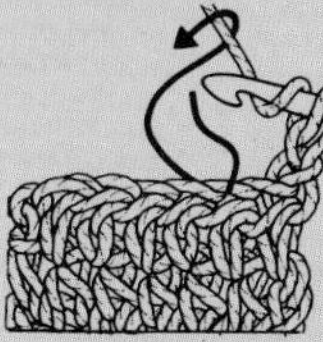

Missing a stitch at each end of row
At beg, t-ch, miss 1st, work next st. At end, miss next to last st, work final st. For double dec, miss 2 sts.

Decreasing several stitches at row ends
At beg, work ss over reqd dec sts, make t-chs, cont in pattern. At end, leave reqd dec sts unworked, make t-chs.

Decreasing in middle of row
Work 2 sts tog as 1. As guide for further dec mark position of dec sts with coloured yarn.

WORKING WITH TWO STITCHES AS ONE

In each case, use the method given below for decreasing in the middle or at the end of a row.

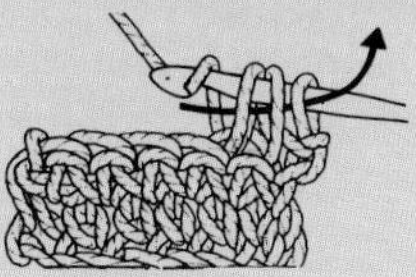

Double crochet
Make t-ch, insert hook into first st, yrh, draw through. Rep into next st, yrh, draw through all lps.

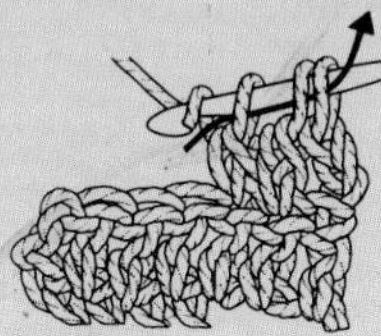

Treble
Make 3 t-ch, yrh, insert hook into first st, draw through, yrh, draw through 2 lps. Rep into next st, yrh, draw through all lps.

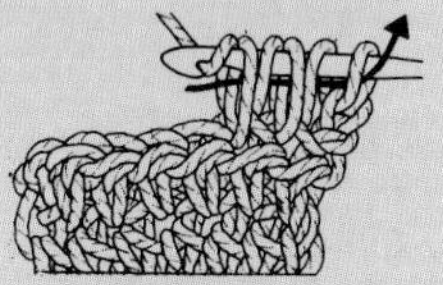

Half treble
Make 2 t-ch. Yrh, insert hook into first st, yrh, draw through. Rep into next st, yrh, draw through all lps.

PUTTING THE STITCH PATTERNS TO USE

Before you begin any crochet work make a tension sample first. This is necessary whether you wish to check your tension measurements against a printed pattern, substitute the suggested stitch or yarn with another, or create a new design.

Making a tension sample
Work a test piece slightly larger than 10 cm square. Lay on a flat surface and mark out the tension measurement given in pattern with pins. Count the rows and stitches between pins. If there are too many stitches between pins try a larger hook; if too few, try a smaller hook.

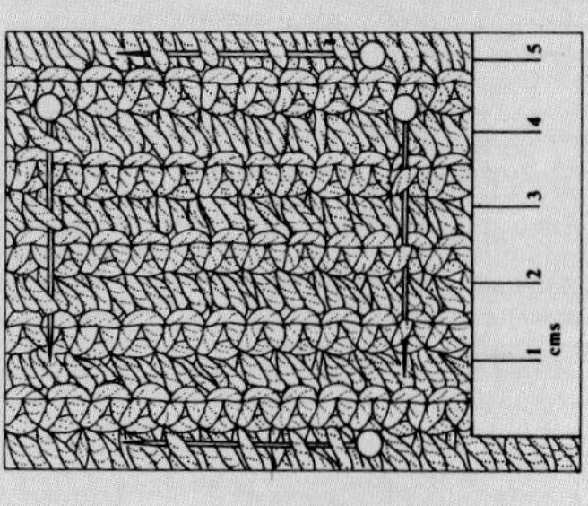

SUBSTITUTING ONE STITCH FOR ANOTHER

Make sure that your substitute stitch is of a similar type to the one suggested in the pattern, and that the stitch multiple will divide evenly into the foundation chain. Stitch multiples in crochet are generally small and can usually be adjusted at the tension sample stage. You may also substitute one yarn for another, providing you choose one from the same group as the original, eg. fine cotton or double knitting yarn, working a tension sample first.

HOOK AND YARN TABLE

0.60 mm	very fine cotton	**4.00**	medium-weight
0.75		**4.50**	double knitting
1.00		**5.00**	yarn
1.25	fine cotton and	**5.50**	double crêpe,
1.50	equivalent yarns	**6.00**	mohair
1.75			
		7.00	Aran-type
2.00	light-weight yarns	**8.00**	double, double yarn
2.50			
3.00		**9.00**	chunky,
3.50		**10.00**	heavy-weight

ABBREVIATIONS

alt	alternate(ly)	**no.**	number
B	back	**patt**	pattern
beg	begin(ning)	**pc**	picot
bet	between	**rem**	remain(ing)
ch(s)	chain(s)	**rep**	repeat
cl	cluster	**reqd**	required
col	colour	**RS**	right side
cont	continu(e)(ing)	**rnd**	round
dec	decreas(e)(ing)	**RTF**	round treble front
dc	double crochet	**ss**	slip stitch
dch(s)	double chain(s)	**sp(s)**	spare(s)
dtr	double treble	**st(s)**	stitch(es)
F	front	**tog**	together
foll	follow(ing)	**tr**	treble
gr(s)	group(s)	**tr tr**	triple treble
htr	half treble	**t-ch(s)**	turning chain(s)
inc	increas(e)(ing)	**WS**	wrong side
lp(s)	loop(s)	**yrh**	yarn round hook

Symbols

A star * shown in a pattern row denotes that the stitches shown after this sign must be repeated from that point.

Round brackets ( ), enclosing a particular stitch combination, denote that the stitch combination must be repeated in the order shown.

Hyphens refer to those stitches which have already been made but which will be used as the base for the next stitch, eg., you would work 2tr into 2-ch sp, by making 2 trebles into the space created by the chain stitches worked in the previous row.

BASIC STITCH PATTERNS

A few simple stitches form the basis of all crochet stitch patterns producing a flat surface and firm fabric (see p.9). Variations to these basic stitches are numerous and include basketweave, cable, ridged and raised effects (see p.11).

Double stitch

Materials Fine rayon or random-dyed yarn for spring wear; medium or heavy-weight wool for a warm, dense-textured fabric.
Uses All-over pattern for waistcoat front, baby's jacket or blanket border; coat or sweater inset panel.

Make any number of ch, 1ch, turn.
Row 1 Insert hook into 2nd ch from hook, yrh, draw lp through, insert hook into next ch, yrh, draw lp through, yrh, draw through all 3 lps on hook, * insert hook into same ch as 2nd lp of previous st, yrh, draw lp through, insert hook into next ch, yrh, draw lp through, yrh, draw through all 3 lps on hook, rep from * to end, 1dc into last st, 1ch, turn.

Row 2 Insert hook into first st, yrh, draw lp through, insert hook into next st, yrh, draw lp through, yrh, draw through all 3 lps on hook, * insert hook into same st as 2nd lp of previous st, yrh, draw lp through, insert hook into next st, yrh, draw lp through, yrh, draw through all 3 lps on hook, rep from * to end, 1dc into last st, 1ch, turn.
Rep row 2 throughout.

Spider stitch

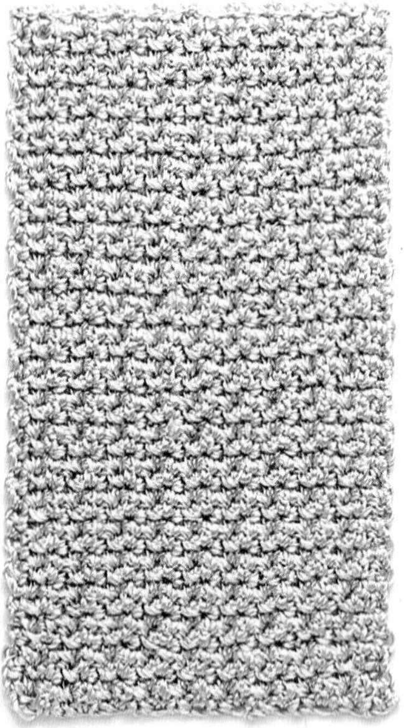

Materials Fine to medium-weight yarn for a pretty, summery look.
Uses Dress yoke or cardigan inset panel; all-over repeat for baby's pram set or small purse.

Make an even number of ch, 2ch, turn.
Row 1 (1dc, 1ch, 1dc) into 3rd ch from hook, * miss 1ch, (1dc, 1ch, 1dc) into next ch, rep from * to last ch, 1dc into last ch, 2ch, turn.
Row 2 * (1dc, 1ch, 1dc) into ch sp, rep from * to end, 1dc into t-ch, 2ch, turn.
Rep row 2 throughout.

Ridged trebles

Materials Chunky or double knitting yarn for a sporty look; medium-weight cotton or lurex for special evening wear.
Uses Sweater inset panel or child's jacket and matching cap; dress yoke or nightie bodice for purchased fabric skirt.

These are also called *stand trebles*.
Make any number of ch, 3ch, turn.
Work a row of tr on foundation ch, 3ch, turn.
Row 1 *1tr into next st, inserting hook through back half only of st, rep from * to end, 3ch, turn.
Rep row 1 throughout.

Ridge stitch

Materials Lightly twisted cotton or synthetic yarn for easy care; chunky or medium yarn for a firm, nubbly fabric.
Uses All-over repeat for beach outfit, bathroom set, cushion or placemat; jacket or dress inset panel.

Make any number of ch, 1ch, turn.
Work a row of dc on foundation ch, 1ch, turn.
Row 1 *1dc into next dc, inserting hook through back half only of st, rep from * to end, 1ch, turn.
Rep row 1 throughout.

Cable stitch

Materials 2- to 4-ply wool for warmth; acrylic or silky yarn for party wear.
Uses Sweater yoke or baby's shawl panel; full-length coat inset band or all-over design for deep V-neck slipover.

Make a number of ch divisible by 4 plus 2, 1ch, turn.
Work a row of dc on foundation ch, 3ch, turn.
Row 1 * Miss next st, 1tr into each of next 3 sts, yrh, insert hook from front to back into the st which was missed and work a tr, rep from * to end, 1tr into t-ch, 1ch, turn.
Row 2 1dc into each st to end, 3ch, turn.
Rep rows 1 and 2 throughout.

Raised trebles

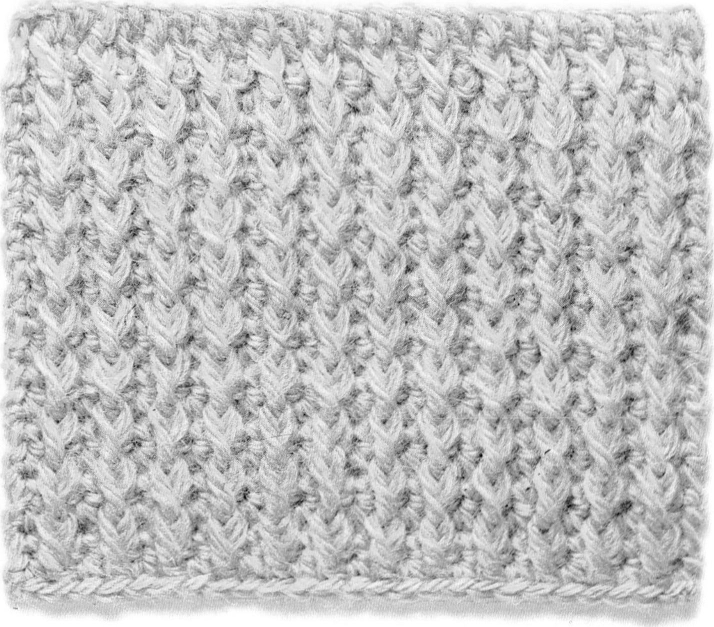

Materials Double knitting wool for warmth; fine to medium-weight yarn for a firm, ridged effect.
Uses Inset panel for father and son cardigan; all-over pattern for sweater, dress bodice or toddler's jacket.

Make an odd number of ch, 3ch, turn. Work a row of tr on foundation ch, 1ch, turn.
Row 1 1dc into each tr to end, 1dc into t-ch, 2ch, turn.
Row 2 * Yrh, keeping hook at front of work, insert hook from right to left round stem of next tr on foundation row and work a tr – called RTF – miss dc above this tr, 1dc into next dc, rep from * to end, ending with 1RTF round stem of last tr, 1dc into t-ch, 1ch, turn.
Row 3 1dc into each st to end, 1dc into t-ch, 2ch, turn.
Row 4 * 1RTF round stem of RTF on row 2, 1dc into next dc, rep from * to end, working last dc into t-ch, 1ch, turn.
Rep rows 3 and 4 throughout.

Crossed half trebles

Materials Medium-weight yarn for a pretty textured look; Shetland or baby wool for softness.
Uses Sweater or blouson jacket inset panel; all-over design for mother and daughter slipover or baby's shawl.

Make an odd number of ch, 2ch, turn.
Row 1 Yrh, insert hook into 3rd ch from hook, yrh, draw lp through, yrh, insert hook into next ch, yrh, draw lp through, yrh, draw through all 5 lps on hook, 1ch, * (yrh, insert hook into next ch, yrh, draw lp through) twice, yrh, draw through all 5 lps on hook, 1ch, rep from * to last ch, 1htr into last ch, 2ch, turn.
Row 2 Yrh, insert hook into first ch sp, yrh, draw lp through, yrh, insert hook into next ch sp, yrh, draw lp through, yrh, draw through all 5 lps on hook, 1ch, * yrh, insert hook into same ch sp as last lp of previous st, yrh, draw lp through, yrh, insert hook into next ch sp, yrh, draw lp through, yrh, draw through all 5 lps on hook, 1ch, rep from * to end, 1htr into t-ch, 2ch, turn.
Rep row 2 throughout.

Basket stitch

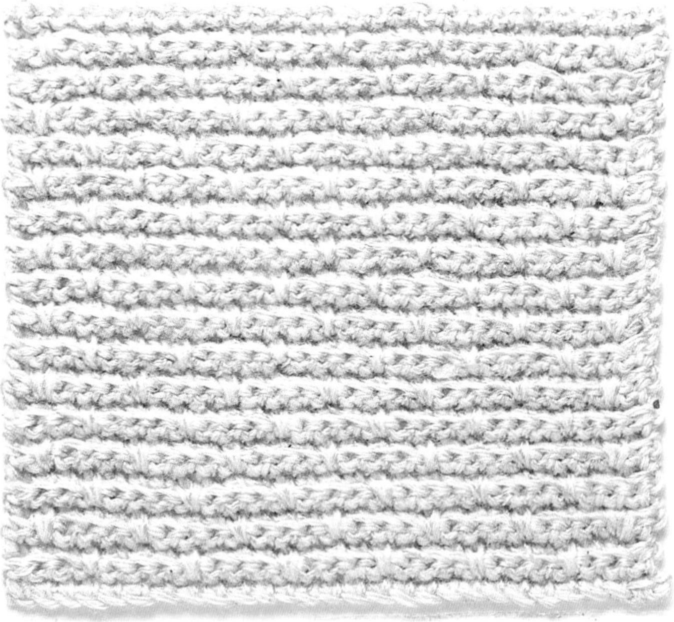

Materials Medium-weight wool or novelty mix for a classic look; random-dyed cotton for beach wear.
Uses Inset band or all-over pattern for button-through cardigan; all-over repeat for bikini or beach blanket border.

Make a number of ch divisible by 4 plus 3, 1ch, turn. Work a row of dc foundation ch, 1ch, turn.
Row 2 *1dc into next dc, inserting hook through back half only of st, rep from * to end, 1ch, turn.
Row 3 1dc into back half of each of first 3dc, * insert hook into st below next dc (i.e. 1 row down) and work a dc, miss this dc, 1dc into back half of next 3dc, rep from * to end, 1ch, turn.
Row 4 1dc into back half of each st to end, 1ch, turn.
Row 5 1dc into back half of first dc, * 1dc into dc below next dc, miss this dc, 1dc into back half of next 3dc, rep from * to last 2 sts, 1dc into dc below next dc, 1dc into back half of last dc, 1ch, turn.
Row 6 As row 4.
Rep rows 3 to 6 throughout.

Textured Patterns

Deeply-textured patterns are made by raising and lowering the fabric in such a way as to create a regular stitch repeat (see p.11). Repeat sizes may be small or large involving a single puffball or cluster; all-over loop, shell and honeycomb designs; or, groups of pineapples or tulips which can be arranged as borders, large spot repeats or all-over patterns.

Raised dots in pineapple stitch

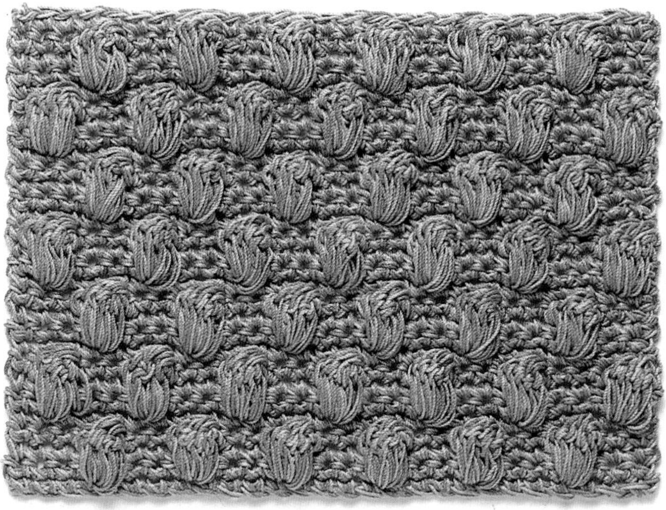

Materials Fine cotton or synthetic yarn for wash and wear; Shetland wool for an Aran effect.
Uses All-over repeat for sleeveless pullover, baby's cot cover or beret; sweater or shawl inset panel.

Make a number of ch divisible by 4 plus 3, 1ch, turn.
Work 3 rows in dc, 1ch, turn.
Row 4 1dc into each of first 3 sts, * insert hook into next st, yrh, draw lp through, (yrh, insert hook into the same st 2 rows below – i.e. first row – yrh, draw lp through, yrh, draw through 2 lps) 6 times, yrh, draw through all 8 lps on hook – called 1 pineapple – 1dc into each of next 3dc, rep from * to end, 1ch, turn.
Work 3 rows in dc, 1ch, turn.
Row 8 1dc into first dc, * 1 pineapple into next dc, 1dc into each of next 3dc, rep from * to last 2 sts, 1 pineapple into next dc, 1dc into next dc, 1ch, turn.
Rep rows 1 to 8 throughout.

Raised diagonal pineapple

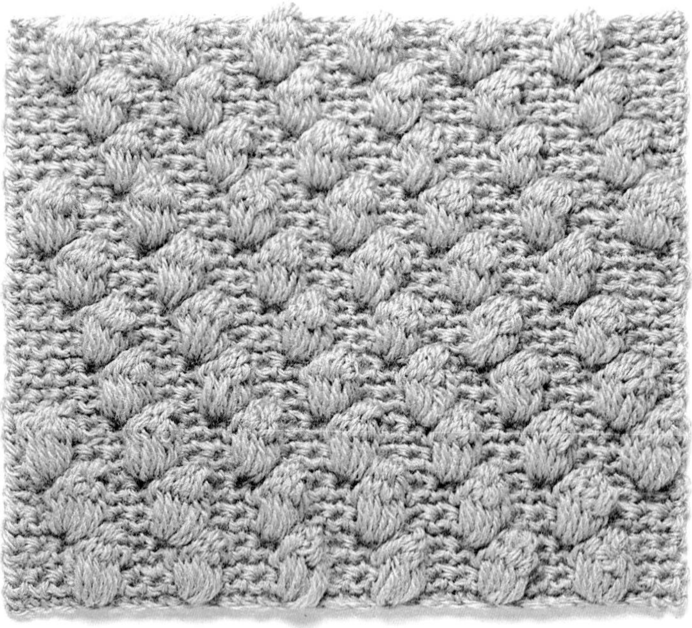

Materials Medium-weight, cotton or acrylic for seaside holiday wear; double knitting wool for Arans.
Uses All-over design for loose-fitting slipover, bed set and bolster; poncho or sweater inset panel.

Make a number of ch divisible by 4 plus 3, 1ch, turn. Work 3 rows in dc, 1ch, turn.
Row 4 1dc into each of first 3 sts, * insert hook into next st, yrh, draw lp through, (yrh, insert hook into the same st 2 rows below – i.e. first row – yrh, draw lp through, yrh, draw through 2 lps) 6 times, yrh, draw through all 8 lps on hook – called 1 pineapple – 1dc into each of next 3dc, rep from * to end, 1ch, turn.
Work 3 rows in dc, 1ch, turn.
Row 8 2dc, * 1 pineapple, 3dc, rep from * to last st, 1 pineapple into last dc, 1ch, turn.
Work 3 rows in dc, 1ch, turn.
Row 12 1dc into first dc, * 1 pineapple into next dc, 1dc into each of next 3dc, rep from * to last 2 sts, 1 pineapple into next dc, 1dc into next dc, 1ch, turn.
Work 3 rows in dc, 1ch, turn.
Row 16 1 pineapple into next st, * 1dc into each of next 3dc, 1 pineapple into next dc, rep from * to last 2 sts, 1dc into each of next 2dc, 1ch, turn.
Rep row 1 to 16 throughout.

Spray stitch

Materials Very fine cotton or silky yarn for special occasions; 2-ply wool for light warmth.
Uses Bridesmaid's purse, party dress insertion or necktie; baby's shawl inset panel, or all-over repeat for bride's cape.

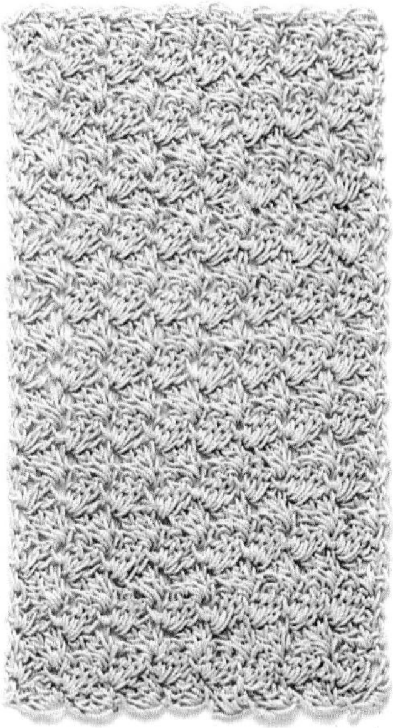

Make a number of ch divisible by 3 plus 1, 2ch, turn.
Row 1 2tr into 3rd ch from hook, * miss 2ch, (1dc, 2tr) into next ch, rep from * to last 3ch, miss 2ch, 1dc into last ch, 2ch, turn.
Row 2 2tr into first dc, *(1dc, 2tr) into next dc, rep from * to end, 1dc into t-ch, 2ch, turn.
Rep row 2 throughout.

Tulip stitch

Materials Medium-weight wool, lurex, silk or rayon yarn for a party look; very fine crochet cotton for sheer daintiness.
Uses All-over pattern for an evening wrap, loose-fitting short waistcoat or pouch bag; edging for print shawl or braces.

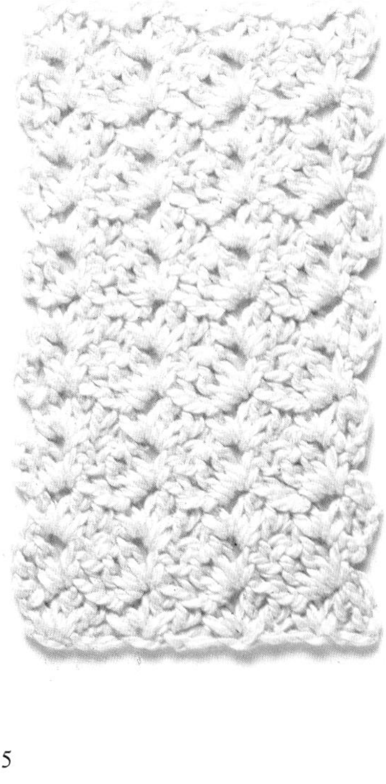

Make a number of ch divisible by 4, plus 1, 3ch, turn.
Row 1 3tr into 4th ch from hook, * miss 3ch, (1dc, 3ch, 3tr) into next ch, rep from * to last 4ch, miss 3ch, 1dc into last ch, 3ch, turn.
Row 2 3tr into first dc, * (1dc, 3ch, 3tr) into 3ch lp, rep from * to last lp, 1dc into last lp, 3ch, turn.
Rep row 2 throughout.

Raised puffballs

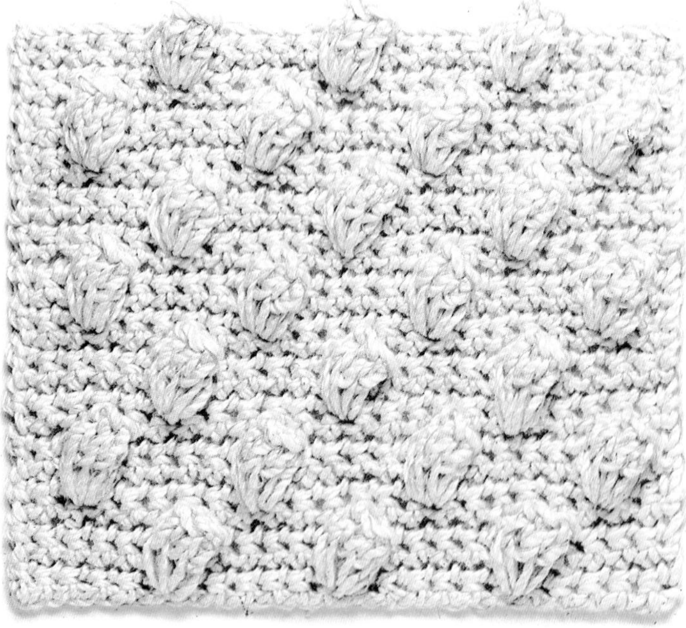

Materials Cotton or synthetic yarn for washability; chunky or double knitting wool for a sporty, Aran look.
Uses Cushion set or hooded blouson jacket; sweater or poncho inset panel; all-over design for bedspread.

Make a number of ch divisible by 6 plus 5, 1ch, turn. Work 3 rows in dc, 1ch, turn.
Row 4 1dc into each of next 5dc, * 1ch, (1tr into next st 2 rows below) 6 times (all into the same st), take hook out of last tr, insert it into the first ch of this gr, pull the lp of the tr through the ch – called puffball – miss this dc, 1dc into each of next 5dc, rep from * to end, 1ch, turn. Work 3 rows in dc, 1ch, turn.
Row 8 1dc into each of first 2dc, * 1ch, 1 puffball below next dc, miss this dc, 1dc into each of next 5dc, rep from * to last 3 sts, 1 puffball below next dc, 1dc into each of last 2dc, 1ch, turn.
Rep rows 1 to 8 throughout.

Blossom stitch

Materials Medium-weight crochet cotton, rayon or fine wool for a close textured fabric.
Uses Cushion, blanket border or straw hat band; sweater or bed-jacket inset panel.

Make a number of ch divisible by 4 plus 3, 2ch, turn.
Row 1 (1tr, 1ch, 1tr) into 3rd ch from hook, miss 1ch, 1dc into next ch, * miss 1ch, (1tr, 1ch, 1tr) into next ch, miss 1ch, 1dc into next ch, rep from * to end, 2ch, turn.
Row 2 * 1tr into dc, 1ch, 1dc into ch sp, 1ch, rep from * to end, 1tr into t-ch, 2ch, turn.
Row 3 * (1tr, 1ch, 1tr) into dc, 1dc into tr, rep from * to end, working last dc into t-ch, 2ch, turn.
Rep rows 2 and 3 throughout.

Rope stitch

Materials Baby wool for softness; fine to medium-weight cotton, lurex or silky yarn for evening wear.
Uses All-over design for shawl or baby's cot cover; camisole top or overblouse inset panel.

Make a number of ch divisible by 3, 3ch, turn.
Row 1 1tr into 4th ch from hook, 1ch, 1tr into next ch, * miss 1ch, 1tr into next ch, 1ch, 1tr into next ch, rep from * to last ch, 1tr into last ch, 3ch, turn.
Row 2 (1tr, 1ch, 1tr) into each ch sp to end, 1tr into t-ch, 3ch, turn.
Rep row 2 throughout.

Honeycomb stitch

Materials 3- to 4-ply wool or double knitting yarn, space-dyed acrylic or novelty mix for casual wear.
Uses Jacket or sweater inset panel or all-over repeat for slipover, beret or blanket square.

Make a number of ch divisible by 3, 1ch, turn.
Work a row of dc on foundation ch, 1ch, turn.
Row 1 *Yrh, insert hook into next st, (yrh, draw lp through, yrh, draw through 2 lps) 5 times, yrh, draw through 6 lps, 1dc into each of next 2dc, rep from * to end, 1ch, turn.
Row 2 1dc into each st to end, 1ch, turn.
Row 3 * 1dc into each of next 2dc, yrh, insert hook into next st, (yrh, draw lp through, yrh, draw through 2 lps) 5 times, yrh, draw through 6 lps, rep from * to end, 1ch, turn.
Row 4 As row 2.
Rep rows 1 to 4 throughout.

Paris stitch

Materials 3- to 4-ply cotton, crêpe or tweedy mix yarn for a classic look.
Uses Dress inset panel, blanket square or all-over pattern for twin-set.

Make a number of ch divisible by 3 plus 1, 3ch, turn.
Row 1 (1tr, 2ch, 1dc) into 4th ch from hook, * miss 2ch, (2tr, 2ch, 1dc) into next ch, rep from * to end, 3ch, turn.
Row 2 (1tr, 2ch, 1dc) into 2ch sp, *(2tr, 2ch, 1dc) into next 2ch sp, rep from * to end, 3ch, turn.
Rep row 2 throughout.

Sweetpea stitch

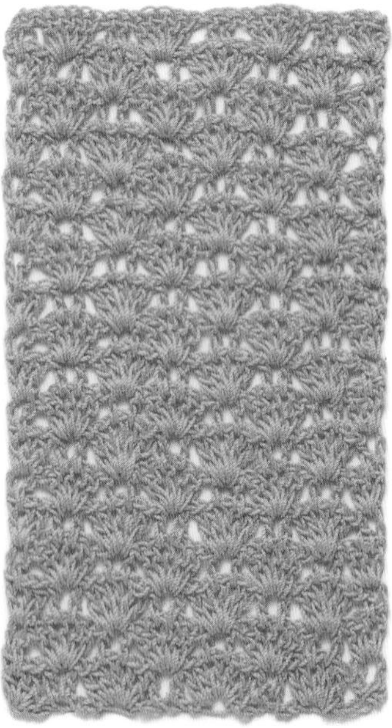

Materials Medium-weight crêpe-rayon, cotton, silk or acrylic yarn for a lacy effect.
Uses Inset panel for child's dress or baby's pram set; all-over design for classic cardigan, sleeveless pullover or dress bodice.

Make a number of ch divisible by 7 plus 4, 3ch, turn.
Row 1 1tr into 4th ch from hook, * miss 2ch, 5tr into next ch, miss 2ch, 1tr into each of next 2ch, rep from * to last 3ch, miss 2ch, 3tr into last ch, 3ch, turn.
Row 2 1tr bet first 2tr, * 5tr bet the 2 single tr, 1tr bet 2nd and 3rd of 5tr, 1tr bet 3rd and 4th of 5tr, rep from * to end, 3tr bet last tr and t-ch, 3ch, turn.
Rep row 2 throughout.

Turtle stitch

Materials Silky yarn or cotton for a softly textured fabric; 3- or 4-ply wool for light warmth.
Uses All-over repeat for loose-fitting waistcoat, silky cravat, necktie or napkin ring; sweater yoke or bedjacket inset panel.

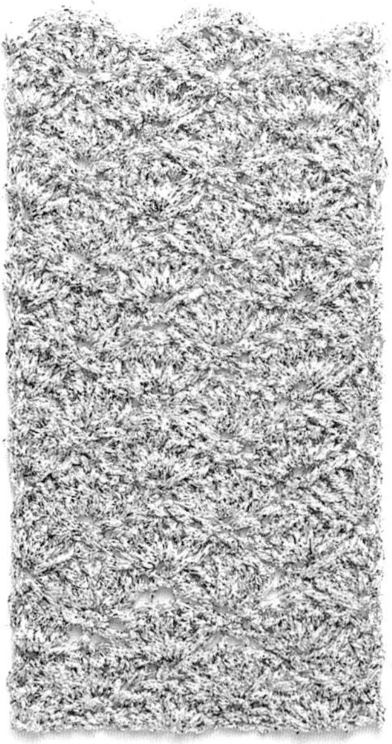

Make a number of ch divisible by 6 plus 4, 3ch, turn.
Row 1 3tr into 4th ch from hook, miss 2ch, 1dc into next ch, * miss 2ch, 5tr into next ch, miss 2ch, 1dc into next ch, rep from * to end, 3ch, turn.
Row 2 Working into the back half only of each st, 3tr into dc, * 1dc into 3rd of 5tr, 5tr into dc, rep from * to end, 1dc into t-ch, 3ch, turn.
Rep row 2 throughout.

Close shell stitch

Materials Cotton or silky yarn for summer wear; 3- to 4-ply yarn or baby wool for light-weight warmth.
Uses All-over design for dress bodice or loose waistcoat; inset panel for baby's jacket or toddler's dress.

Make a number of ch divisible by 6, plus 4, 3ch, turn.
Row 1 3tr into 4th ch from hook, miss 2ch, 1dc into next ch, * miss 2ch, 4tr into next ch, miss 2ch, 1dc into next ch, rep from * to end, 3ch, turn.
Row 2 2tr into dc, * 1dc bet 2nd and 3rd tr, 4tr into dc, rep from * to end, 1dc bet last tr and t-ch, 3ch, turn.
Rep row 2 throughout.

Parquet stitch

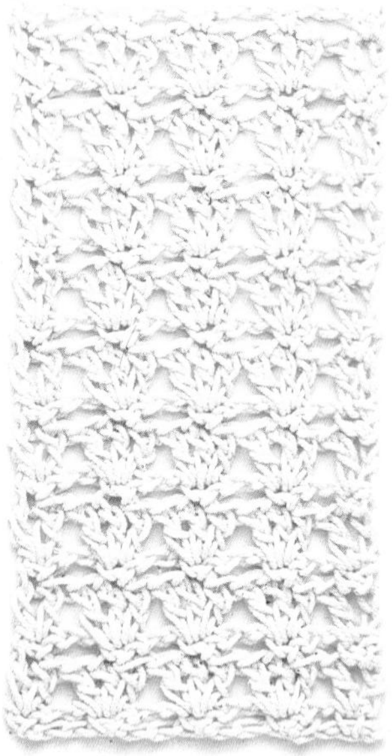

Materials Fine to medium-weight cotton or acrylic for wash and wear; lurex or silky yarn for a summery look.
Uses Bag inset panel, yoke band and shoulder ties for print dress; all-over design for slipover, ribbon-threaded evening purse or buffet runner.

Make a number of ch divisible by 3 plus 1, 1ch, turn.
Row 1 1dc into 2nd ch from hook, * 2ch, miss 2ch, 1dc into next ch, rep from * to end, 3ch, turn.
Row 2 1tr into first dc, * 3tr into next dc, rep from * to end, 2tr into last dc, 1ch, turn.
Row 3 1dc into first tr, * 2ch, 1dc into 2nd of 3tr, rep from * to end, 2ch, 1dc into t-ch, 3ch, turn.
Rep rows 2 and 3 throughout.

Loop stitch

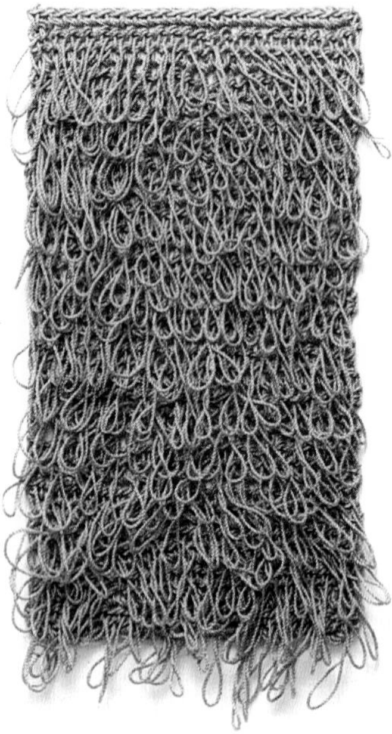

Materials Cotton or synthetic yarn for easy care; 4-ply yarn, double knitting or chenille for warmth.
Uses Jacket trim or all-over pattern for bathroom set; all-over repeat for full-length coat and beret, egg or teapot cosy, pram cover or furry toys.

Make any number of ch, 1ch, turn. Work a row of dc on the foundation ch, 1ch, turn.
Row 1 (wrong side of work) * Yrh, insert hook into next st, take yarn round finger, yrh, draw lp through, yrh, draw through 3 lps on hook, rep from * to end, 1ch, turn.
Row 2 1dc into each st to end, 1ch, turn.
Rep rows 1 and 2 throughout.

Colour Patterns

Many attractive and intricate effects can be crocheted simply by introducing two or more colours into patterns (see p.12). As the technique for working colour patterns produces a close fabric, it is generally advisable to use a hook one size larger than the normal choice for the chosen yarn. Patterns vary from a single dot repeat through speckle and petal patterns to undulating peaks and pinnacles.

Dot stitch

Materials Fine to medium-weight yarn for a two-tone ermine effect.
Uses Front inset panel for classic twinset or all-over pattern for boy or girl sleeveless pullover, gloves or hat.

This pattern uses 2 colours, A and B.
Using A, make a number of ch divisible by 3 plus 1, 1ch, turn.
Row 1 1dc into 2nd ch from hook, *2ch, miss 2ch, 1dc into next ch, rep from * to end, joining in B on last dc.
Row 2 Using B, 4ch, *3tr into 2ch sp, 1ch, rep from * to end, 1tr into last dc.
Row 3 Return to beg of row 2, draw A through under 4th of 4ch, 1ch as first dc, *2ch, 1dc into 1ch sp, rep from * to end, drawing B through on last dc.
Row 4 Using B, work as row 2. Always starting each row at the end where the correct colour was left, rep rows 3 and 4 throughout.

Brick stitch

Materials Medium to heavy-weight yarn for a pebbly textured, warm fabric.
Uses Edge detail for knitted cardigan or all-over design for a toddler's first coat, family sweaters or cushion set.

This pattern uses 3 colours, A, B and C.
Using A, make a number of ch divisible by 4 plus 2, 2ch, turn.
Row 1 1tr into 4th ch from hook, * 2ch, miss 2ch, 1tr into each of next 2ch, rep from * to end, joining in B on last tr.
Row 2 Using B, 2ch, *1tr into each of the 2 missed ch on row 1, 2ch, rep from * to end, ending with 1ch instead of 2, then ss into 3rd of 3ch at beg of row 1, joining in C.
Row 3 Using C, 3ch, 1tr into missed tr on last row, *2ch, 1tr into each of 2 missed tr on last row, rep from * to end, drawing A through on last tr.
Row 4 Using A, work as row 2.
Working 1 row in each colour throughout rep rows 3 and 4.

Almond stitch

Materials Chunky yarn for warmth; double knitting or tweedy mix for a sporty look.
Uses Jacket inset band; all-over pattern for lady's golf sweater or family slippers.

This stitch uses 2 colours, A and B.
Using A make a number of ch divisible by 10 plus 1, 1ch, turn.
Row 1 1dc into 2nd ch from hook 1dc into each ch to end, joining in B on last dc.
Row 2 Using B, 1ch, *1dc into next st, 1htr into next st, 1tr into each of next 5 sts, 1htr into next st, 1dc into next st, 1ch, miss 1 st, rep from * to end, ss into t-ch, turn.
Row 3 Using B, 1ch, *1dc into dc, 1htr into htr, 1tr into each of 5tr, 1htr into htr, 1dc into dc, 1ch, rep from * to end, ss into t-ch, drawing A through.
Row 4 3ch, *1dc into each of next 9 sts, 1tr into missed st of row 1, rep from * to end, ending with 1 tr into t-ch.
Row 5 Using A, 1ch, 1dc into each st to end, drawing through B on last dc.
Row 6 Using B, 3ch, 1tr into each of next 2 sts, *1htr into next st, 1dc into next st, 1ch, miss 1st, 1dc into next st, 1htr into next st, 1tr into each of next 5 sts, rep from * to end, but ending with 3tr instead of 5.
Row 7 3ch, 1tr into each of next 2tr, *1htr into htr, 1dc into dc, 1ch, 1dc into dc, 1htr into htr, 1tr into each of 5tr, rep from * to end, but ending with 3tr instead of 5 and draw through A on last tr.
Row 8 Using A, 1ch as first dc, 1dc into each of next 4 sts, *1tr into miss st of row 5, 1dc into each of next 9 sts, rep from * to end, but ending with 1dc into each of next 5 sts.
Row 9 As row 5.
Rep rows 2 to 9 throughout.

Pinnacle stitch

Materials Shetland, double knitting wool or mohair for warmth or for a figure-flattering fabric.
Uses All-over repeat for throwover bedspread, shaded cushion set or travel rug; dress or skirt, shawl or scarf border.

This pattern uses 2 colours, A and B.
Using A, make a number of ch divisible by 14 plus 1, 2ch, turn.
Row 1 1dc into 3rd ch from hook, *1dc into each of next 5ch, miss 3ch, 1dc into each of next 5ch, 3dc into next ch, rep from * to end, but ending with 2dc into last ch instead of 3.

Row 2 1ch, 1dc into same place, * 1dc into each of next 5dc, miss 2dc, 1dc into each of next 5dc, 3dc into next dc, rep from * to end, but ending with 2dc into t-ch.
Rep row 2 throughout, working 2 more rows in A, then 4 rows in B and 4 rows in A throughout.

Petal stitch

Materials Medium-weight wool, silk, crêpe or acrylic yarn for softness; crochet cotton for a finer fabric.
Uses Dress yoke, slipover inset panel or all-over pattern for bed-jacket or shawl; scatter cushion border, deep collar and cuffs or waistcoat trim.

This pattern uses 2 colours, A and B.
Using A make a number of ch divisible by 6 plus 1, 3ch, turn.
Row 1 2tr into 4th ch from hook, * miss 2ch, 1dc into next ch, miss 2ch, 5tr into next ch, rep from * to end, ending with 3tr into last ch instead of 5.
Row 2 Join B to top of 3ch at beg of row 1, 1dc into this st, *2ch, ** yrh, insert hook into next tr, yrh, draw lp through, yrh, draw through 2 lps ** rep from ** to ** into next tr, into dc, then into each of next 2tr, yrh, draw through 6 lps on hook, 2ch, 1dc into next tr, rep from * to end, drawing through A on last dc.
Row 3 Using A, 3ch, 2tr into first dc, *1dc into top of gr, 5tr into next dc, rep from * to end, but ending with 3tr into last dc.
Row 4 Return to beg of row 3, draw B through top of 3ch and work as row 2.
Rep rows 3 and 4 throughout.

Speckle stitch

Materials Medium-weight wool or synthetic yarn for a rich tweedy effect.
Uses Mother and daughter sweater inset panel or all-over pattern for man's sleeveless cardigan or deerstalker cap.

This pattern uses 3 colours, A, B and C.
Using A, make a number of ch divisible by 3 plus 2, 1ch, turn.
Row 1 1dc into 3rd ch from hook, 1dc into each ch to end.
Row 2 1ch, 1dc, into each dc to end. Do not break off A.
Row 3 Join in B, 1ch, 1dc into each dc to end.
Row 4 As row 2. Do not break off B.
Row 5 Return to beg of row 4, join in C, 1ch, 1dc into each dc to end. Do not break off C.
Row 6 Draw A through first st, 1ch, 1dc into next dc, *1dtr inserting hook from right to left in front of corresponding st on row 2, 1dc into each of next 2dc, rep from * to end.
Row 7 As row 2.
Row 8 Draw C through first st, 1ch, 1dc into each dc to end.
Row 9 Return to beg of row 8, draw B through first st, 1ch, 1dc into next dc, *1dtr, inserting hook from right to left in front of dtr on row 6, 1dc into each of next 2dc, rep from * to end.
Row 10 As row 2.
Always starting each row at the correct end where yarn was left, rep rows 5 to 10 throughout.

OPENWORK

Open work stitch patterns are some of the quickest and easiest to crochet (see p.12). As all openwork is made by leaving large spaces between stitches, the work grows rapidly. This group of lacy stitch patterns, combined with the variety of crochet yarns available, offers one of the widest ranges of decorative textures – from a simple net ground, arch, picot and knot to intricate crown and peacock patterns.

Simple net ground

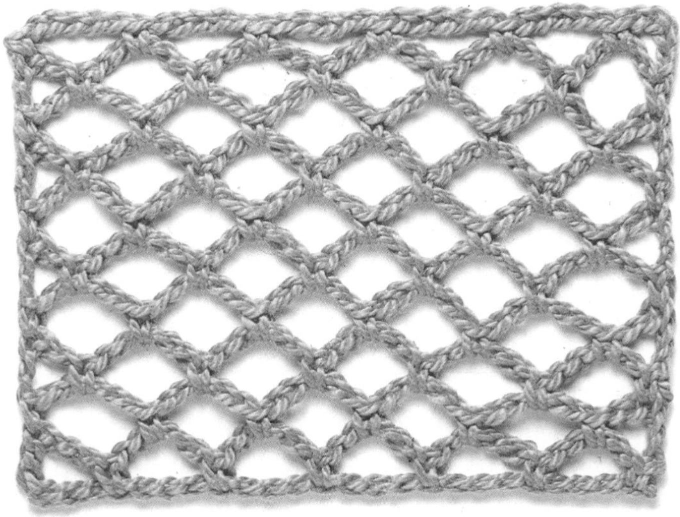

Materials Cotton for easy care; very fine wool, silk or lurex for special evening wear.
Uses All-over pattern for loose-fitting slipover or beach bag; shimmery shawl or dress and jacket inset panel.

Make a number of ch divisible by 4 plus 1, 5ch, turn.
Row 1 1dc into 10th ch from hook, * 5ch, miss 3ch, 1dc into next ch, rep from * to end, 5ch, turn.
Row 2 1dc into 5ch lp, * 5ch, 1dc into next lp, rep from * to end, 5ch, turn.
Rep row 2 throughout.

Solomon's knot

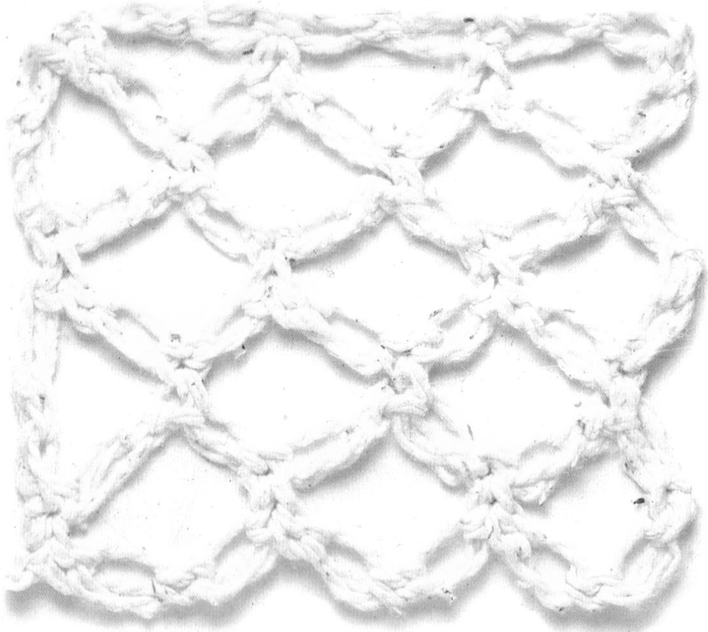

Materials Medium-weight dishcloth cotton, bouclé yarn or mohair for softness; fine string, tubular rayon or russia braid for furnishing.
Uses All-over pattern for curtain room divider, scarf or shawl; shopping bag, applied border for lampshade, woven bedspread or rug trim.

There is no foundation ch for this stitch. Make a slip lp and put onto hook.
Row 1 *Draw lp up to 1.3cm, yrh, draw lp through, insert hook bet double and single threads of lp just made, yrh, draw lp through, yrh, draw through both lps on hook, rep from * for length reqd, making an even no. of knots, turn.
Row 2 Miss knot on hook and next 3 knots, work 1dc into next knot, * make 2 knots as on row 1, miss 1 knot on row 1, work 1dc into next knot, rep from * to end, working last dc into first ch on row 1.
Row 3 Make 3 knots, 1dc into next free knot along last row, * make 2 knots, 1dc into next free knot along last row, rep from * to end.
Rep row 3 throughout.

Bar and lattice

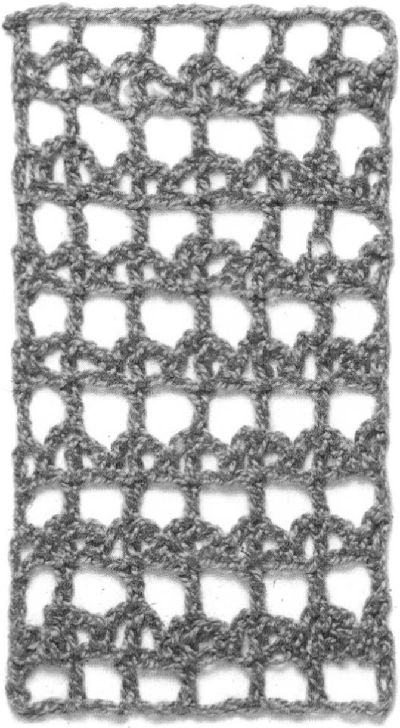

Materials Fine to medium-weight wool for a dressy effect; cotton or synthetic yarn for a cool look.
Uses Ribbon-threaded dress yoke or inset panel; all-over pattern for café curtain.

Make a number of ch divisible by 4 plus 1, 5ch, turn.
Row 1 1tr into 10th ch from hook, * 3ch, miss 3ch, 1tr into next ch, rep from * to end, 4ch, turn.
Row 2 * 1dc into 2nd of 3ch, 2ch, 1tr into tr, 2ch, rep from * to end, ending with 2dc into 2nd ch, 2ch, 1tr into t-ch, 5ch, turn.
Row 3 1tr into next tr, * 3ch, 1tr into next tr, rep from * to end, working last tr into t-ch, 4ch, turn.
Rep rows 2 and 3 throughout.

Star stitch

Materials Fine wool, silk crêpe or rayon for a soft, pretty look; medium-weight yarn, soft string or lurex for a rich textured effect.
Uses Dress inset panel or shawl border; all-over repeat for button-through cardigan, cushion set or bedspread border.

Make a number of ch divisible by 4 plus 1, 3ch, turn.
Row 1 1tr into 8th ch from hook, (1ch, 1tr) 3 times into same ch, * miss 3ch, 1tr into next ch, (1ch, 1tr) 3 times into same ch, rep from * to last 4ch, miss 3ch, 1tr into last ch, 3ch, turn.
Row 2 * 1tr into 2nd ch sp of shell, (1ch, 1tr) 3 times into same ch sp, rep from * to end, 1tr into t-ch, 3ch, turn.
Rep row 2 throughout.

Picot lace ground

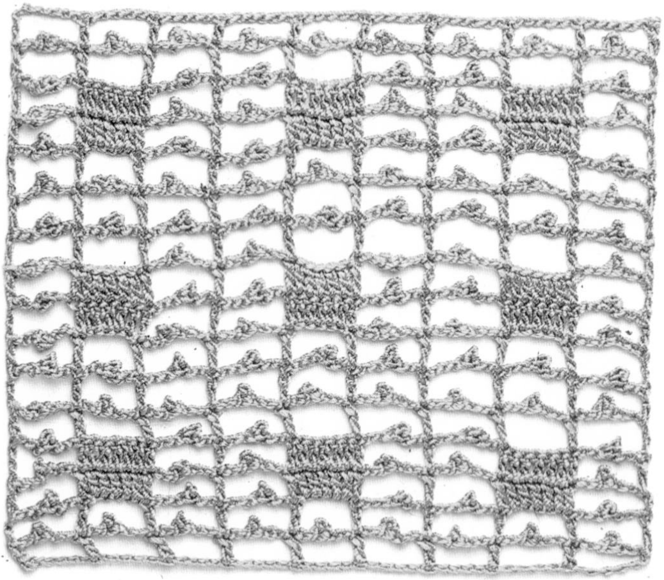

Materials Medium-weight mohair for a winter wedding; silk or lurex for a special party look.
Uses All-over pattern for bride's lacy wrap; glittery triangular shawl, lacy cravat or beaded sash.

Make a number of ch divisible by 15 plus 1, 7ch, turn.
Row 1 1dc into 3rd ch from hook – called picot – 2ch, miss 9ch, 1tr into next ch, * 5ch, pc, 2ch, miss 4ch, 1tr into next ch, rep from * to end, 8ch, pc, 2ch, turn.
Row 2 Miss first tr, 1tr into next tr, * 5ch, 1tr into next tr, (5ch, pc, 2ch, 1tr into next tr) twice, rep from * to last 2pc, 5ch, 1tr into next tr, 5ch, pc, 2ch, 1tr into 3rd ch beyond pc, 8ch, pc, 2ch, turn.
Row 3 Miss first tr, 1tr into next tr, * 1tr into each of next 5ch, 1tr into next tr, (5ch, pc, 2ch, 1tr into next tr) twice, rep from * ending with 1tr into each of next 5ch, 1tr into next tr, 5ch, pc, 2ch, 1tr into 3rd ch beyond pc, 8ch, pc, 2ch, turn.
Row 4 Miss first tr, 1tr into next tr, * 1tr into each of next 6tr, (5ch, pc, 2ch, 1tr into next tr) twice, rep from * ending with 1tr into each of next 6tr, 5ch, pc, 2ch, 1tr into 3rd ch beyond pc, 8ch, pc, 2ch, turn.
Row 5 Miss first tr, 1tr into next tr, * 5ch, pc, 2ch, miss 5tr, 1tr into next tr, (5ch, pc, 2ch, 1tr into next tr) twice, rep from * ending with 5ch, pc, 2ch, miss 5tr, 1tr into next tr, 5ch, pc, 2ch, 1tr into 3rd ch beyond pc, 8ch, pc, 2ch, turn.
Row 6 Miss first tr, 1tr into next tr, * 5ch, pc, 2ch, 1tr into next tr, rep from * to end, working last tr into 3rd ch beyond pc, 8ch, pc, 2ch, turn.
Rep rows 2 to 6 throughout.

Ladder stitch

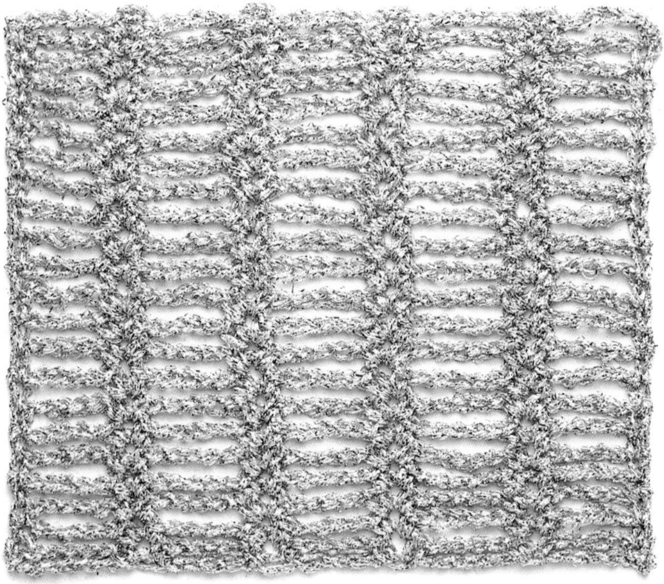

Materials Cotton for sunshine, lurex for moonlight; double knitting wool, mohair or angora for warmth.
Uses All-over pattern for beach wrap or blouson, cape or camisole top; jerkin, long, belted cardigan or scarf.

Make a number of ch divisible by 6 plus 1, 1ch, turn.
Row 1 1dc into 2nd ch from hook, * 5ch, miss 5ch, (1dc, 3ch, 1dc) into next ch, rep from * to last 6ch, 5ch, miss 5ch, 1dc into last ch, 1ch, turn.

Row 2 1dc into first dc, * 5ch, (1dc, 3ch, 1dc) into 3ch lp, rep from * to end, ending with 5ch, 1dc into last dc, 1ch, turn.
Rep row 2 throughout.

Diamond stitch

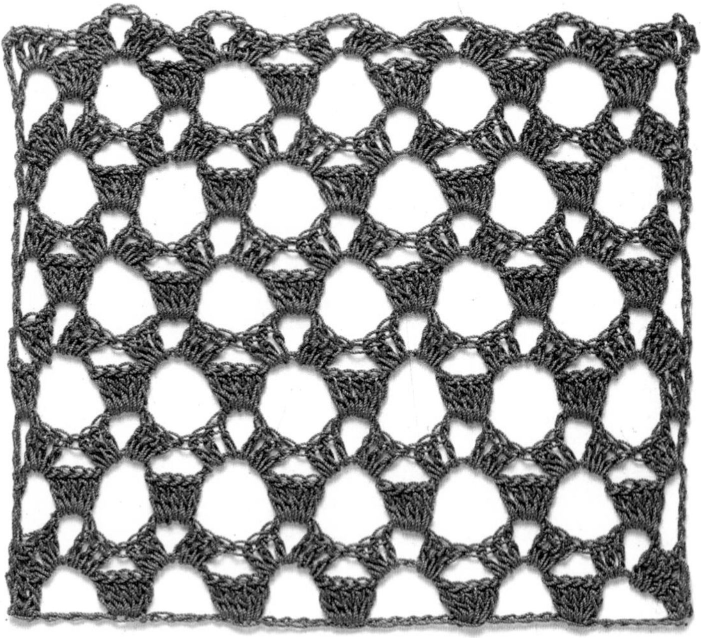

Materials Perle cotton, synthetic yarn, slub linen or dishcloth cotton for easy care.
Uses Cushion border, bedcover flounce with added fringe or all-over repeat for lunch mat.

Make a number of ch divisible by 6 plus 1, 3ch, turn.
Row 1 2tr into 4th ch from hook, * 4ch, miss 5ch, 5tr into next ch, rep from * to last 6ch, 4ch, miss 5ch, 3tr into last ch, 1ch, turn.
Row 2 * (3tr, 3ch, 3tr) into 4ch sp, rep from * to end, 1dc into t-ch, 6ch, turn.
Row 3 * 5tr into 3ch sp, 4ch, rep from * to end, ending with 5tr into 3ch sp, 3ch, 1tr into t-ch, 5ch, turn.
Row 4 3tr into 3ch sp, * (3tr, 3ch, 3tr) into 4ch sp, rep from * to end, ending with (3tr, 2ch, 1tr) into t-ch, 3ch, turn.
Row 5 2tr into 2ch sp, * 4ch, 5tr into 3ch sp, rep from * to end, 4ch, 3tr into t-ch, 1ch, turn.
Rep rows 2 to 5 throughout.

Reseau stitch

Materials Silk, rayon or cotton yarn for summer wear; chunky or double knitting wool for warmth.
Uses Evening wrap or shawl inset panel; all-over repeat for blanket with contrast needle-weaving using fur strips or thick wool.

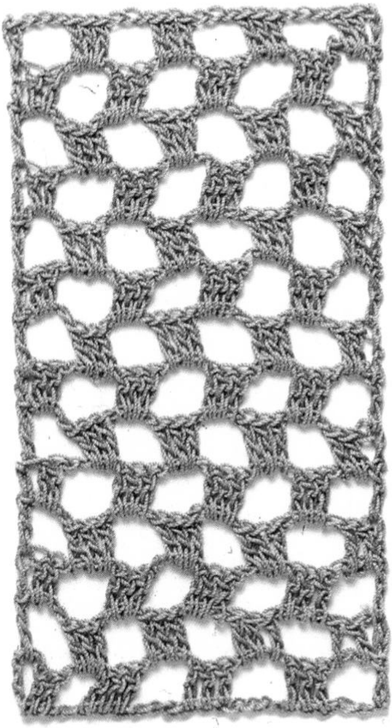

Make a number of ch divisible by 6 plus 1, 3ch, turn.
Row 1 1tr into 4th ch from hook, 1tr into next ch, * 3ch, miss 3ch, 1tr into each of next 3ch, rep from * to last 4ch, 3ch, miss 3ch, 1tr into last ch, 3ch, turn.
Row 2 2tr into first 3ch sp, * 3ch, 3tr into next 3ch sp, rep from * to end, ending with 3ch, 1tr into t-ch, 3ch, turn.
Rep row 2 throughout.

Irish net stitch

Materials Fine crochet cotton for a lacy look; medium-weight yarn for furnishing.
Uses All-over pattern for classic-style cardigan; combine with Irish motifs into all-over pattern for bedcover or buffet runner.

Make a number of ch divisible by 4 plus 1, 5ch, turn.
Row 1 (1dc, 3ch, 1dc) into 10th ch from hook, * 5ch, miss 3ch, (1dc, 3ch, 1dc) into next ch, rep from * to last 4ch, 5ch, miss 3ch, 1dc into last ch, 5ch, turn.
Row 2 * (1dc, 3ch, 1dc) into 3rd of 5ch, 5ch, rep from * to end, 1dc into t-ch, 5ch, turn.
Rep row 2 throughout.

Crown stitch

Materials Soft cotton, silky crêpe or lurex for an extra pretty look; fine baby wool for lightness.
Uses Dress yoke or inset band; christening shawl inset border or all-over pattern for baby's pram set.

Make a number of ch divisible by 7 plus 2, 2ch, turn.
Row 1 1htr into 3rd ch from hook, 1htr into next ch, * 3ch, miss 2ch, 1dc into next ch, 3ch, miss 2ch, 1htr into each of next 2ch, rep from * to end, 2ch, turn.
Row 2 1htr into each of first 2htr, * 3ch, (1dc, 3ch, 1dc) into dc, 3ch, 1htr into each of next 2htr, rep from * to end, 1ch, turn.
Row 3 1dc into each of 2htr, * 1dc into 3ch sp, 5ch, 1dc into next 3ch sp, 1dc into each of 2htr, rep from * to end, 1ch, turn.
Row 4 1dc into each of first 2dc, * miss 1dc, 7dc into 5ch sp, miss 1dc, 1dc into each of next 2dc, rep from * to end, 2ch, turn.
Row 5 1htr into each of first 2dc, * 3ch, miss 3dc, 1dc into next dc, 3ch, miss 3dc, 1htr into each of next 2dc, rep from * to end, 2ch, turn.
Rep rows 2 to 5 throughout.

Peacock stitch

Materials Medium-weight cotton or acrylic for wash and wear; Shetland wool or mohair for lacy softness.
Uses Bedspread or curtain border; shawl inset panel, loose-fitting blouson top or scarf.

Make a number of ch divisible by 14 plus 1, 1ch, turn.
Row 1 1dc into 2nd ch from hook, * miss 6ch, 13 long tr into next ch (drawing lp up to 1.3cm to form a long tr), miss 6ch, 1dc into next ch, rep from * to end, 4ch, turn.
Row 2 1 long tr into dc, * 5ch, 1dc into 7th of 13 long tr, 5ch, 2 long tr into dc, rep from * to end, 1ch, turn.
Row 3 * 1dc bet 2 long tr, 13 long tr into dc, rep from * to end, 1dc bet long tr and t-ch, 4ch, turn.
Rep rows 2 and 3 throughout.

Ruby lace ground

Materials Fine Shetland wool, cotton or synthetic yarn for a light lacy effect.

Uses Shawl inset panel, woven dress sleeve and bodice insertion or all-over pattern for bedcover border.

Make a number of ch divisible by 8, 1ch, turn.

Row 1 Starting into 2nd ch from hook, * 1dc into next 4ch, 3ch, ss into first of these 3ch – called picot – 1dc into each of next 4ch, turn, 9ch, ss to first dc, turn, into the 9ch lp work 7dc, 3pc, 7dc, rep from * to end, 9ch, turn.

Row 2 * 1dc into 2nd of 3pc, 8ch, rep from * to end, 1dc into 2nd of 3pc, 4ch, 1tr tr into t-ch, 1ch, turn.

Row 3 1dc into each of next 4ch, turn, 5ch, ss to first dc, turn, 2pc, 7dc into 5ch lp, rep from * on first row to last 9ch, 1dc into each of next 4ch, turn, 5ch, ss into first dc, turn, 7dc into 5ch lp, 2pc, turn.

Row 4 * 8ch, 1dc into 2nd of 3pc, rep from * to end, 3ch, turn.

Rep rows 1 to 4 throughout.

COLOURWORK

Patterns using two or more colours in a row are easier to read if charted on graph paper (one square equals one stitch). Read charts upwards from right-hand corner. Bring second colour yarn in by drawing it through last two loops of first colour, and vice versa, keeping yarn not in use on wrong side (see p.12).

Zigzags

Materials Chunky or double knitting yarn for warmth; medium-weight cotton for sun wear.
Uses Kimono-style jacket or child's dressing gown inset panel; all-over pattern for swimsuit, bikini or beach mat.

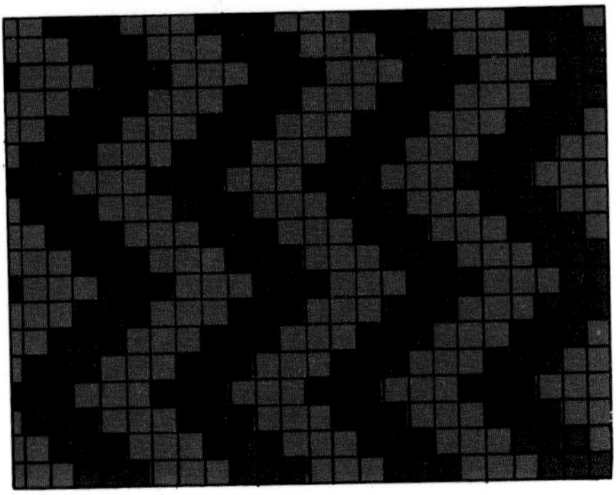

Repeat:
6 sts × 8 rows

Horizontal stripes

Materials Medium-weight yarn for a sporty finish; 1cm wide fabric strips for economy furnishing.
Uses All-over pattern for loose-fitting blazer or square-neck sweater; kitchen cushion or hearth rug.

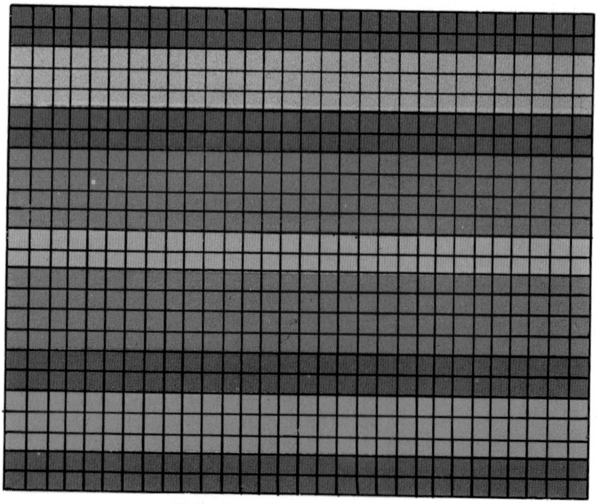

Repeat: 1 st × 24 rows

Vertical stripes

Materials 4-ply wool or novelty yarn for casual wear.
Uses Inset panel for mother and daughter button-through cardigan or man's waistcoat front; all-over repeat for patchwork blanket or scarf.

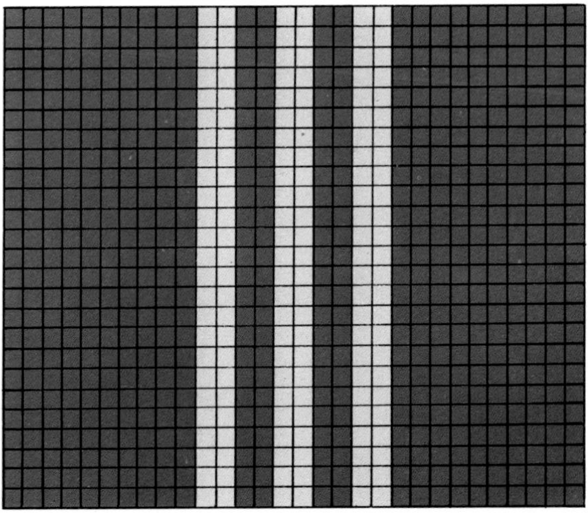

Repeat: 18 sts × 1 row

Diamonds

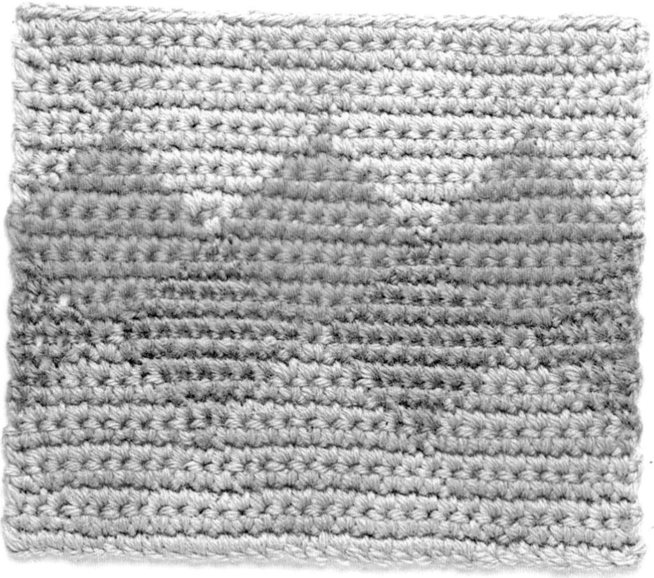

Materials Medium-weight wool or tweedy mix for snug warmth; cotton yarn for easy care.
Uses Father and son jacket inset panel, sweater band or bedroom slippers; bathroom set or shoulder bag border.

Repeat: 10 sts × 20 rows

Plain Medallions

Crochet is easily made into circles or squares by working in the round and increasing at regular intervals (see p.14). As each row is worked from the same side, there is no right or wrong side to the fabric. Medallion patterns may be plain, close-stitched, or a mixture of both.

Arcade diamond

Materials Fine wool for a lacy finish; random-dyed cotton for a softly mottled look.
Uses Join together for throwover bedspread or shawl; baby carrier, curtain or placemat.

Make 6ch and join into a ring with a ss into first ch.
Round 1 3ch, 15tr into ring, join with a ss to 3rd of first 3ch.
Round 2 5ch, * 1tr into next tr, 2ch, rep from * 14 times more, join with a ss to 3rd of first 5ch.
Round 3 Ss into first sp, 3ch, (1tr, 3ch, 2tr) into same sp, * (2ch, 1dc into next sp) 3 times, 2ch, (2tr, 3ch, 2tr) into next sp, rep from * twice more, (2ch, 1dc into next sp) 3 times, 2ch, join with a ss to 3rd of first 3ch.
Round 4 Ss into next 3ch sp, 3ch, (1tr, 3ch, 2tr) into same sp, * (2ch, 1dc into 2ch sp) 4 times, 2ch, (2tr, 3ch, 2tr) into 3ch sp, rep from * twice more, (2ch, 1dc into 2ch sp) 4 times, 2ch, join with a ss to 3rd of first 3ch.
Round 5 Ss into 3ch sp, 3ch, (2tr, 2ch, 3tr) into same sp, * (1ch, 2tr into 2ch sp) 5 times, 1ch, (3tr, 2ch, 3tr) into 3ch sp, rep from * twice more, (1ch, 2tr into 2ch sp) 5 times, 1ch, join with a ss to 3rd of first 3ch. Fasten off.

Framed square

Materials Medium-weight yarn for warmth; jute and a jumbo hook for furnishing.
Uses Motif for potholder, coaster or all-over repeat for patchwork coverlet; casserole stand, or enlarge motif for doormat.

Make 8ch and join into a ring with a ss into first ch.
Round 1 3ch, 15tr into ring, join with a ss to 3rd of first 3ch.
Round 2 5ch, (1tr into next tr, 2ch) 15 times, join with a ss to 3rd of first 5ch.
Round 3 Ss into first 2ch sp, 3ch, 2tr into same sp, 1ch, * 3tr into next sp, 1ch, rep from * to end, join with a ss to 3rd of first 3ch.
Round 4 Ss into first ch sp, * (3ch, 1dc into next sp) 3 times, 6ch, 1dc into next sp, rep from * 3 times more, omitting last dc and join with a ss to ss at beg of rnd.
Round 5 Ss into first 3ch sp, 3ch, 2tr into same sp, 3tr into each of next 2 3ch sps, * (5tr, 2ch, 5tr) into 6ch sp, 3tr into each of next 3 3ch sps, rep from * twice more, (5tr, 2ch, 5tr) into 6ch sp, join with a ss to 3rd of first 3ch.
Round 6 3ch, 1tr into each tr to corner, * (1tr, 1dtr, 1tr) into 2ch sp, 1tr into each tr to next corner, rep from * twice more, (1tr, 1dtr, 1tr) into 2ch sp, 1tr into each tr to end, join with a ss to 3rd of first 3ch.
Fasten off.

Primula circle

Materials Double knitting yarn for appliqué; very fine crochet cotton or silk for an extra special finish.
Uses Spot motif or posy pattern for sweater decoration; applied motif for wedding dress or veil, baby's christening gown or a lapel badge.

Make 4ch and join into a ring with a ss into first ch.
Round 1 1ch, 11dc into ring, join with a ss to first ch.
Round 2 1ch, 1dc into same place, inserting hook into back half of each st work 2dc into each st to end, join with a ss to first ch.
Round 3 3ch, * miss 1dc, 1dc into back half of next dc, 2ch, rep from * to end, join with a ss to first of first 3ch.
Round 4 Into each 2ch sp work 1dc, 1tr, 2dtr, 1tr and 1dc, join with a ss to first dc.
Fasten off.

Scalloped circle

Materials Fine to medium-weight crêpe, rayon or cotton for a lacy look.
Uses Single motifs for applying to bridesmaid's ribbon sash or hairslide; all-over repeat for placemat, tablecloth or bedspread.

Make 6ch and join into a ring with a ss into first ch.
Round 1 3ch, 23tr into ring, join with a ss to 3rd of first 3ch.
Round 2 5ch, 1tr into ss, 1ch, * miss 2tr, (1tr, 2ch, 1tr) into next tr, 1ch, rep from * 6 times more, join with a ss to 3rd of first 5ch.
Round 3 Ss into 2ch sp, 3ch, (1tr, 2ch, 2tr) into same sp, * 1dc into 1ch sp, (2tr, 2ch, 2tr) into 2ch sp, rep from * 6 times more, 1dc into 1ch sp, join with a ss into 3rd of first 3ch.
Round 4 Ss into 2ch sp, 3ch, (2tr, 1ch, 3tr) into same sp, * 1dc before next dc, 1dc after the same dc, (3tr, 1ch, 3tr) into 2ch sp, rep from * 6 times more, 1dc before next dc, 1dc after the same dc, join with a ss to 3rd of first 3ch.
Fasten off.

Plain hexagon

Materials 4-ply wool, double knitting or acrylic yarn for light warmth; cotton or rayon yarn for wash and wear.
Uses Join medallions for plain or patchwork shawl, blanket, waistcoat or hot water-bottle cover; single motif for placemat or coaster.

Make 4ch and join into a ring with a ss into first ch.
Round 1 1ch, 11dc into ring, join with a ss to first ch, turn.
Round 2 2ch, * 3htr into next dc, 1htr into next dc, rep from * 4 times more, 3htr into next dc, join with a ss to 2nd of first 2ch, turn.
Round 3 2ch, 1htr into next htr, * 3htr into next htr, 1htr into each of next 3htr, rep from * 4 times more, 3htr into next htr, 1htr into next htr, join with a ss to 2nd of first 2ch, turn.
Round 4 2ch, 1htr into each of next 2htr, * 3htr into next htr, 1htr into each of next 5htr, rep from * 4 times more, 3htr into next htr, 1htr into each of next 2htr, join with a ss to 2nd of first 2ch, turn.
Cont in this way, working 2 more htr along each side in each rnd until hexagon is the required size. Fasten off.

Spiral hexagon

Materials Medium-weight yarn or space-dyed cotton for town wear; fine string for a country look.
Uses Beret, bedspread and bolster module, or scatter cushion; drawstring bag base or hot pot stand.

Make 5ch and join into a ring with a ss into first ch.
Round 1 * 6ch, 1dc into ring, rep from * 5 times more, ss over first 3ch of first lp.
Round 2 * 4ch, 1dc into 6ch lp, rep from * 5 times more, working the last dc into ss before the first 4ch.
Round 3 * 4ch, 2dc into 4ch lp, 1dc into dc, rep from * 5 times more, working last dc into last dc at end of last rnd.
Round 4 * 4ch, 2dc into 4ch lp, 1dc into each of next 2dc, rep from * to end.
Round 5 * 4ch, 2dc into 4ch lp, 1dc into each of next 3dc, rep from * to end.
Cont in this way, working 1 more dc in each group on each rnd until motif is the required size, ending with a ss into next dc.
Fasten off.

Flower hexagon

Materials Medium-weight yarn for country furnishing; raffia for cottage kitchen wear.
Uses Patchwork blanket module or pillow panel; cooking pot stand or placemat.

Make 6ch and join into a ring with a ss into first ch.
Round 1 4ch, (1tr into ring, 1ch) 11 times, join with a ss to 3rd of first 4ch.
Round 2 3ch, 2tr into sp, 1tr into tr, 2ch, * 1tr into tr, 2tr into sp, 1tr into tr, 2ch, rep from * 4 times more, join with a ss to 3rd of first 3ch.
Round 3 3ch, 1tr into same place, 1tr into each of next 2tr, 2tr into next tr, 2ch, * 2tr into next tr, 1tr into each of next 2tr, 2tr into next tr, 2ch, rep from * 4 times more, join with a ss to 3rd of first 3ch.
Round 4 3ch, 1tr into same place, 1tr into each of next 4tr, 2tr into next tr, 2ch, * 2tr into next tr, 1tr into each of next 4tr, 2tr into next tr, 2ch, rep from * 4 times more, join with a ss to 3rd of first 3ch.
Round 5 3ch, 1tr into each of next 7tr, * 3ch, 1dc into 2ch sp, 3ch, 1tr into each of next 8tr, rep from * 4 times more, 3ch, 1dc into 2ch sp, 3ch, join with a ss to 3rd of first 3ch.
Round 6 Ss into next tr, 3ch, 1tr into each of next 5tr, * 3ch, (1dc into 3ch sp, 3ch) twice, miss next tr, 1tr into each of next 6tr, rep from * 4 times more, 3ch, (1dc into 3ch sp, 3ch) twice, join with a ss to 3rd of first 3ch.
Round 7 Ss into next tr, 3ch, 1tr into each of next 3tr, * 3ch, (1dc into 3ch sp, 3ch) 3 times, miss next tr, 1tr into each of next 4tr, rep from * 4 times more, 3ch, (1dc into 3ch sp, 3ch) 3 times, join with a ss to 3rd of first 3ch.
Round 8 Ss between 2nd and 3rd tr of group, 3ch, 1tr into same place, * 3ch, (1dc into 3ch sp, 3ch) 4 times, 2tr between 2nd and 3rd tr of gr, rep from * 4 times more, 3ch, (1dc into 3ch sp, 3ch) 4 times, join with a ss to 3rd of first 3ch.
Round 9 Ss into 3ch sp, 3ch, 3tr into same sp, (4tr into 3ch sp) 4 times, * 3ch, miss 2tr, (4tr into 3ch sp) 5 times, rep from * 4 times more, 3ch, join with a ss to 3rd of first 3ch.
Fasten off.

Lace Medallions

By working chains and large spaces into a decorative motif, lacy medallions are quickly and easily made. Alternatively, separate motifs can be made and the lace mesh background worked around them. Lace medallion patterns include both stylized and natural forms, geometric designs and cobwebby net grounds. Insert medallions singly or join together to form a border, panel or all-over repeat.

Willow lace square

Materials Fine cotton, rayon or silky yarn for a pretty lace look.
Uses All-over square or diamond repeat for shawl, tablecloth, buffet runner or throwover lampshade cover.

Make 5ch and join into a ring with a ss into first ch.
Round 1 1ch, 11dc into ring, ss to first ch.
Round 2 * 15ch, ss into next dc, rep from * 11 times more, working last ss into ss at end of rnd 1.
Round 3 Ss along to centre of first lp, * 4ch, 1dc into next lp, 4ch, (yrh, insert hook into next lp, yrh, draw lp through, yrh, draw through 2 lps) 3 times, yrh, draw through all 4 lps on hook – called cluster – 4ch, cl into same lp, 4ch, 1dc into next lp, rep from * 3 times more, working last dc into ss at beg of rnd.
Round 4 Ss along to centre of first 4ch lp, 3ch, cl into this same lp, * 4ch, 1dc into next lp, 4ch, (cl, 4ch, cl) into next lp, 4ch, 1dc into next lp, 4ch, cl into next lp, rep from * 3 times more, but omit last cl and ss to 3rd of first 3ch.
Fasten off.

Irish lace square

Materials Fine to medium-weight rayon, cotton or lurex for an overall lacy effect.
Uses All-over repeat for bedcover, window pelmet, cushion panel or shimmery evening jacket.

Make 16ch.
Round 1 1dc into first of the 16ch, to make a lp, (15ch, 1dc into same ch as before) twice. 3 lps now made.
Round 2 24dc into each lp, join with a ss to first dc.
Round 3 1dc into each dc all round, join with a ss to first dc.
Round 4 Ss into each of next 3dc, * 1dc into next dc, ** 4ch, 1dc into 3rd ch from hook, 5ch, 1dc into 3rd ch from hook, 1ch ** – called 1 picot loop – miss 4dc, 1dc into next dc, (1 picot loop, miss 4dc, 1dc into next dc) twice, 1 picot lp, 1dc into 5th dc of next leaf, rep from * twice more, omitting the last dc and working a ss into first dc of rnd. 12 picot lps now made.
Round 5 Ss along to centre of first picot lp, * 8ch, 1dc into centre of next lp, turn, ss into lp just made, 3ch, 9tr into same lp, 1tr into next dc, turn, 4ch, miss first 2tr, 1tr into next tr, (1ch, miss 1tr, 1tr into next tr) 3 times, 1ch, miss 1tr, 1tr into 3rd of 3ch, 4ch, 1dc into 3rd ch from hook, 2ch, 1dc into same lp, (1 picot lp, 1dc into centre of next lp) twice, rep from * 3 times more, but omitting last dc and working a ss into ss at base of first 8ch.
Round 6 Ss up side of tr and into each of next 3ch, * 1 picot lp, 1dc into centre 1ch sp, 1 picot lp, 1dc into last tr of "crown" (1 picot lp, 1dc into centre of next lp) twice, 1 picot lp, 1dc into 3rd of 3ch at beg of "crown", rep from * 3 times more, omitting last dc and working a ss into ss before first picot lp.
Round 7 Ss along to centre of first picot lp, work as rnd 5, but working 4 picot lps between each "crown" instead of 2.
Round 8 As rnd 6 but working 2 more picot lps along each side of square.
Fasten off.

COLOUR MEDALLIONS

With one or two exceptions colour medallions are worked in the round where each new colour is joined at the beginning of a round (see p.12). Many small medallions can be made from yarn oddments and joined in an all-over repeat, or at random, into a large multi-colour blanket, rug or bedspread. Other medallions, such as America and Alpine squares may be increased into cushion or rug sizes simply by adding more rows in colour sequence.

Ridged square

Materials Chunky, double knitting or synthetic yarn for a warm, lacy effect; wool oddments for cost cutting.
Uses Border for knitted afghan or woven shawl; all-over pattern for blanket or cushion.

This square uses 5 colours, A, B, C, D and E.
Using A, make 8ch and join into a ring with a ss.
Round 1 4ch, 3dtr into ring, * 5ch, 4dtr into ring, rep from * twice more, 5ch, join with a ss to 4th of first 4ch.
Fasten off.

Make 3 more squares in the same way, one each in B, C and D.
Using E, join squares thus: place 2 squares tog with wrong sides tog, join E to 1 corner, work 3dc into sp, 1dc bet each dtr, 3dc into sp.
Fasten off.

Wheel square

Materials Double knitting, mohair or bouclé yarn for a tweedy look; random-dyed for a mottled effect.
Uses Waistcoat inset panel or blanket square; all-over design for a baby's hooded cape or cot cover.

This uses 2 colours, A and B.
Using A, make 8ch and join into a ring with a ss into first ch.
Round 1 Using A, 6ch, * 1tr into ring, 3ch, rep from * 6 times more, join with a ss to 3rd of first 6ch. Break off A.
Round 2 Join in B to any sp, 3ch, 3tr into same sp, * 2ch, 4tr into next sp, rep from * 6 times more, 2ch, join with a ss to 3rd of first 3ch. Break off B.
Round 3 Join in A to any sp, 3ch, 5tr into same sp, * 1ch, 6tr into next sp, 3ch, 6tr into next sp, rep from * twice more, 1ch, 6tr into next sp, 3ch, join with a ss to 3rd of first 3ch. Break off A.
Round 4 Join in B to a 1ch sp, * 3ch, 1dc between 3rd and 4th tr of gr, 3ch, (2tr, 3ch, 2tr) into 3ch sp, 3ch, 1dc bet 3rd and 4th tr of gr, 3ch, 1dc into 1ch sp, rep from * 3 times more, omitting last dc and join with a ss to first ch.
Fasten off.

Begonia square

Materials Chunky or double knitting wool for warmth; medium-weight cotton or synthetic yarn for light furnishing.
Uses All-over patchwork repeat for poncho or coverlet; café curtain, room divider or stepped-edge table cover.

This uses 2 colours, A and B.
Using A, make 4ch and join into a ring with a ss into first ch.
Round 1 Using A, 4ch, ** yrh twice, insert hook into ring, yrh, draw lp through, (yrh, draw through 2 lps) twice ** rep from ** to ** 3 times more, yrh, draw through 5 lps, * 4ch, rep from ** to ** 5 times, yrh, draw through 6 lps, rep from * 6 times more, 4ch, join with a ss to 4th of first 4ch. Break off A.
Round 2 Join in B to a 4ch lp, 3ch, 3tr into same sp, * 4tr into next sp, 6ch, 4tr into next sp, rep from * twice more, 4tr into next sp, 6ch, join with a ss to 3rd of first 3ch.
Fasten off.

Star hexagon

Materials Chunky wool for bedsitter furnishing.
Uses All-over pattern for patchwork blanket and cushion set.

This motif uses 3 colours, A, B and C.

Using A, make 6ch and join into a ring with a ss into first ch.

Round 1 4ch, 2dtr into ring, * 1ch, 3dtr into ring, rep from * 4 times more, 1ch, join with a ss to 4th of first 4ch, turn.

Round 2 Using A, * 1dc into 1ch sp, 7ch, rep from * 5 times more, join with a ss to first dc. Break off A.

Round 3 Join B to a 7ch lp, into each lp work 1htr, 2tr, 3dtr, 2tr, 1htr, join with a ss to first htr. Break off B.

Round 4 Join C to first htr of a petal, 4ch, 1tr into each of 2tr, 1htr into each of 3dtr, 1tr into each of 2tr, 1dtr into htr, * 1dtr into htr, 1tr into each of 2tr, 1htr into each of 3dtr, 1tr into each of 2tr, 1dtr into htr, rep from * 4 times more, join with a ss to 4th of first 4ch.

Fasten off.

American square

Materials Chunky yarn for country-style furnishing; 4-ply novelty mix, bouclé or mohair for budget fashion.
Uses All-over patchwork repeat for fringed rug, bedspread or pillow; poncho, triangular shawl or waistcoat inset panel.

This square uses 2 colours, A and B.
Using A, make 6ch and join into a ring with a ss into first ch.
Round 1 Using A, 3ch, 2tr into ring, * 3ch, 3tr into ring, rep from * twice more, 3ch, join with a ss to 3rd of first 3ch. Break off A.
Round 2 Join in B to any sp, 3ch, (2tr, 3ch, 3tr) into same sp, * 1ch, (3tr, 3ch, 3tr) into next sp, rep from * twice more, 1ch, join with a ss to 3rd of first 3ch. Break off B.
Round 3 Join in A to a 3ch sp, 3ch, (2tr, 3ch, 3tr) into same sp, * 1ch, 3tr into 1ch sp, 1ch, (3tr, 3ch, 3tr) into 3ch sp, rep from * twice more, 1ch, 3tr into 1ch sp, 1ch, join with a ss to 3rd of first 3ch. Break off A.
Round 4 Join in B to a 3ch sp, 3ch, (2tr, 3ch, 3tr) into same sp, * (1ch, 3tr into 1ch sp) twice, 1ch, (3tr, 3ch, 3tr) into 3ch sp, rep from * twice more, (1ch, 3tr into 1ch sp) twice, 1ch, join with a ss to 3rd of first 3ch.
Fasten off.

Mosaic octagon

Materials Very fine crochet cotton, silk or lurex for extra delicate finery; medium-weight cotton or acrylic yarn for furnishing.
Uses Border detail for wedding veil or spot repeat for net dress; placemat or pot holder motif or all-over design for octagonal tablecloth.

This uses 2 colours, A and B.
Using A, make 6ch and join into a ring with a ss into first ch.
Round 1 Using A, 3ch, 15tr into ring, join with a ss to 3rd of first 3ch. Break off A.
Round 2 Join B to any tr, 3ch, (1tr, 1ch, 2tr) into same place, * miss 1tr, (2tr, 1ch, 2tr) into next tr, rep from * 6 times more, join with a ss to 3rd of first 3ch.
Break off B.
Round 3 Join A to a 1ch sp, 3ch, (1tr, 1ch, 2tr) into same sp, * 1tr bet gr, (2tr, 1ch, 2tr) into 1ch sp, rep from * 6 times more, 1tr bet gr, join with a ss to 3rd of first 3ch. Break off A.
Round 4 Join B to any st, 1ch, 1dc into each st all round, join with a ss to first ch.
Fasten off.

Tricolour square

Materials Lightly twisted 4-ply yarn for extra softness; pastel shades for baby wear.
Uses All-over pattern for bright afghan blanket or full-length hooded coat and scarf; pram cover or baby carrier.

This square uses 3 colours, A, B and C.
Using A, make 8ch and join into a ring with a ss into first ch.
Round 1 Using A, 4ch, 5dtr into ring, * 3ch, 6dtr into ring, rep from * twice more, 3ch, join with a ss to 4th of first 4ch.
Round 2 Using A, 5ch, ** yrh twice, insert hook into next dtr, yrh, draw lp through, (yrh, draw through 2 lps) twice, ** rep from ** to ** into each of next 4dtr, yrh, draw through 6 lps, * 5ch, 1ss into 2nd of 3ch, 5ch, rep from ** to ** into each of next 6dtr, yrh, draw through 7 lps, rep from * twice more, 5ch, 1ss into 2nd of 3ch. Break off A.
Round 3 Join in B to top of a cl, * work (3dtr, 1ch, 3dtr, 2ch, 3dtr, 1ch, 3dtr) into 3ch sp of rnd 1, 1ss into top of next cl, rep from * 3 times more, working last ss into same place as yarn was joined, and joining in A at the same time. Break off B.
Round 4 Using A, 4ch, 5dtr into same ss, * (6dtr, 2ch, 6dtr) into 2ch sp, 6dtr into ss at top of next cl, rep from * twice more, (6dtr, 2ch, 6dtr) into 2ch sp, join with a ss to 4th of first 4ch. Break off A.
Round 5 Join in C to last ss of rnd 4, 1ch, 1dc into each of next 5dtr, 1tr into 1ch sp between gr of dtr on rnd 3, * 1dc into each of next 6dtr, 3dc into 2ch sp at corner, (1dc into each of next 6dtr, 1tr into 1ch sp bet gr of dtr on rnd 3) twice, rep from * twice more, 1dc into each of next 6dtr, 3dc into 2ch sp at corner, 1dc into each of next 6dtr, 1tr into 1ch sp bet gr of dtr on rnd 3, join with a ss to first ch.
Round 6 Using C, 3ch, 1tr into each st all round, working 3tr into centre st of each corner, end by joining with a ss to 3rd of first 3ch.
Fasten off.

Lotus circle

Materials Medium-weight wool or synthetic mix for snug warmth; dishcloth string for easy care.
Uses Join in patchwork pattern for throwover bedspread, cushion set or beret; single motif for pot holder or bag base.

This motif uses 2 colours, A and B.
Make 3ch in A and join into a ring with a ss into first ch.
Round 1 1ch, 7dc into ring, join with a ss to first ch.
Round 2 1ch, join in B and work 1dc into same place, * 1dc in A and 1dc in B into next st, rep from * to end, join with a ss in A into first ch.
Round 3 1ch, working into the back half only of each st on *every* rnd, * 2dc in B into next dc, 1dc in A into next dc, rep from * to last st, 2dc in B into last st, join with a ss in A into first ch.
Round 4 1ch, * 2dc in B into next dc, 1dc in B into next dc, 1dc in A into next dc, rep from * to last 2 sts, 2dc in B into next dc, 1dc in B into next dc, join with a ss in A to first ch.
Round 5 1ch, * 2dc in B into next dc, 1dc in B into each of next 2dc, 1dc in A into next dc, rep from * to last 3 sts, 2dc in B into next dc, 1dc in B into each of next 2dc, join with a ss in A into first ch.
Cont in this way, working 1 more st in B in each gr on every rnd until there are 8 sts in B in each gr (63 sts in the rnd).
Round 10 1ch, * 2dc in A into next dc, 1dc in B into each of next 7dc, 1dc in A into next dc, rep from * to end, but omit the last dc in A and join with a ss in A into first ch.
Round 11 1ch, * 2dc in A into next dc, 1dc in A into each of next 2dc, 1dc in B into each of next 6dc, 1dc in A into next dc, rep from * to end, but omit the last dc in A and join with a ss in A into first ch.
Cont in this way, still inc 7 sts in every rnd, but working 1 st less in B in each gr on every rnd until only 1 st in B remains (112 sts in the rnd).
Fasten off.

Alpen square

Materials Medium-weight yarn oddments for economy; space-dyed 4-ply or acrylic yarn for a soft, shaded effect.
Uses Combine with contrast repeat for bedspread, jerkin or poncho; all-over pattern for hooded baby carrier or cot cover.

This square uses 4 colours, A, B, C and D.
Using A, make 6ch and join into a ring with a ss into first ch.
Round 1 Using A, 1ch, 15dc into ring, join with a ss to first ch.
Round 2 Using A, 11ch, * miss 3dc, 1dc into next dc, 10ch, rep from * twice more, join with a ss to first of first 11ch.
Round 3 Using A, 1ch, * 11dc into 10ch lp, 1dc into dc, rep from * 3 times more, but omit last dc and join with a ss to first ch. Break off A.
Round 4 Join in B to 6th of 11dc, 1ch, 1dc into same place, 1dc into each dc all round and 1dc, 1ch, 1dc into each corner, join with a ss to first ch. Break off B.
Round 5 Join in C to corner and work as rnd 4. Break off C.
Round 6 Join in D to corner and work as rnd 4. Break off D.
Cont in the same way, working 1 rnd in C, then 2 rnds in A.
Fasten off.

Two-tone hexagon

Materials Chunky yarn oddments for budget brightness; a jumbo hook and fine rope or sisal for cottage-style furnishing.
Uses All-over repeat for hexagonal sofa blanket, cushion set or cape; enlarged motif for doormat or kitchen rug.

This motif uses 2 colours, A and B.
Using A, make 6ch and join into a ring with a ss into first ch.
Round 1 Using A, 3ch, 2tr into ring, * 3ch, 3tr into ring, rep from * 4 times more, 3ch, join with a ss to 3rd of first 3ch. Break off A.
Round 2 Join B to 3ch sp, 5ch, (2tr tr, 2ch, 3tr tr) into same sp, * (3tr tr, 2ch, 3tr tr) into next sp, rep from * 4 times more, join with a ss to 5th of first 5ch. Break off B.
Round 3 Join A to same place as ss, 3ch, 1tr into each of next 2tr tr, * (2tr, 2ch, 2tr) into 2ch sp, 1tr into each of next 6tr tr, rep from * 4 times more, (2tr, 2ch, 2tr) into 2ch sp, 1tr into each of next 3tr tr, join with a ss to 3rd of first 3ch. Break off A.
Round 4 Join B into any st, 3ch, 1tr into previous st, * miss 1 st, 1tr into next st, 1tr into the missed st, rep from * all round, join with a ss to 3rd of first 3ch. Fasten off.

Relief Motifs

Three-dimensional medallions are made by using the bobble or embossed technique (see p.11), or by working twice into the same round. Motifs range from tiny flowers to large geometric patterns. Apply medallions singly or join in an all-over repeat.

Looped nosegay

Materials Medium-weight cotton or fine wool for a deep pile effect.
Uses Combine with contrast patterns into blanket square, cushion set or wall panel decoration.

This medallion uses 3 colours, A, B and C.
Using A, make 3ch and join into a ring with a ss into first ch.
Round 1 1ch, 3dc into ring, ss into first ch.
Round 2 1ch, 1dc into same place, 2dc into each dc to end, ss into first ch.
Round 3 As rnd 2. Break off A.
Round 4 Join in B, 1ch, * 2dc into next dc, 1dc into next dc, rep from * 7 times more, but omit last dc and work a ss into first ch. Break off B.
Round 5 Join in C, 1ch, * 2dc into next dc, 1dc into each of next 2dc, rep from * 7 times more, but omit last dc and work a ss into first ch.
Round 6 Using C, 1ch, * 2dc into next dc, 1dc into each of next 3dc, rep from * 7 times more, ending as before. Break off C.
Round 7 Turn work and join in A with wrong side facing, 1ch, * yrh, insert hook into next st, hold a pencil behind work and take the yarn round it to form a loop, yrh, draw lp through, yrh, draw through 3 lps on hook, rep from * to end, ss to first ch. Break off A.
Round 8 Join in B and work as rnd 7, but inc 8 sts evenly in the round. Break off B.
Round 9 Join in C and work as rnd 8.
Fasten off.

Magnolia

Materials Soft, loosely twisted cotton, rayon or fine wool for a three-dimensional finish.
Uses Spot repeat for sweater, party dress border, haircomb trim, bedroom cushion set or guest towel posy motif.

This medallion uses 3 colours, A, B and C.
Using A, make 5ch and join into a ring with a ss into first ch.
Round 1 1ch, 4dc into ring, ss to first ch.
Round 2 1ch, 1dc into same place, 2dc into each dc to end, ss to first ch.
Round 3 2ch, 1htr into same place, 2htr into each dc to end, ss to 2nd of first 2ch.
Round 4 Inserting hook into front strand only of each st, * 3ch, 1dtr into same place, 2dtr into each of next 2htr, (1dtr, 3ch, 1ss) into next htr, 1ss into next htr, rep from * 4 times more. Break off A.
Round 5 Join B behind the centre of one petal, then inserting hook into back strand only of each st of rnd 4, work as rnd 4 but working tr tr instead of dtr. Break off B.
Round 6 Join C in *front* of work into a dc of rnd 1, (3ch, 1dc into next dc) 4 times, 3ch, ss into same place as join.
Fasten off.

Cineraria

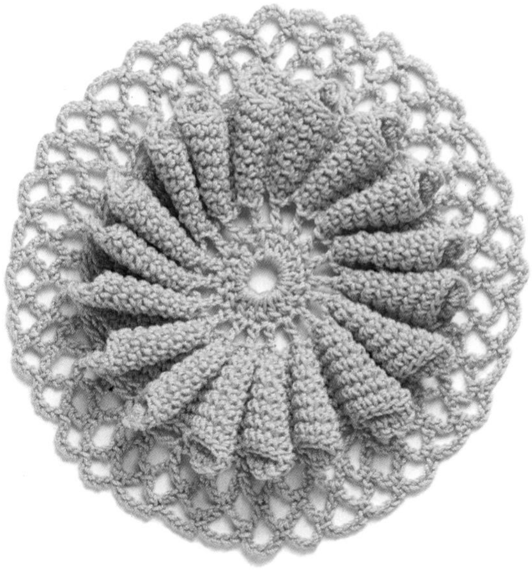

Materials Fine crochet cotton, linen thread or rayon mix for a firm textured effect.
Uses Spot repeat for counterpane squares and matching bolster or hat brim decoration.

Make 8ch and join into a ring with a ss into first ch.
Round 1 3ch, 17tr into ring, ss into 3rd of 3ch.
Round 2 8ch, (1tr into next tr, 5ch) 17 times, ss into 3rd of first 8ch.
Round 3 * 1dc into each of next 2ch, (1dc, 1ch, 1dc) into next ch, 1dc into each of next 2ch, miss 1tr, rep from * 17 times more.
Round 4 * 1dc into each of next 3dc, (1dc, 1ch, 1dc) into 1ch sp, 1dc into each of next 3dc, rep from * 17 times more.
Rounds 5, 6, 7, 8 and 9 As rnd 4, working one more dc in each gr on each round.
Round 10 * 5ch, 1dc bet 8th and 9th of next 16dc (i.e., above the tr which was missed in rnd 3) rep from * 16 times more, 5ch, ss into base of first 5ch.
Round 11 * 5ch, 1dc into 3rd ch of lp, 5ch, 1dc into next dc, rep from * 17 times more, omitting last dc and working a ss into base of first 5ch.
Round 12 Ss along to 3rd ch of lp, * 5ch, 1dc into next lp, rep from * 35 times more, omitting last dc and working a ss into ss before first 5ch.
Round 13 As rnd 12.
Fasten off.

Bobble square

Materials Medium-weight cotton or rayon, plain or random-dyed acrylic or synthetic mix for wash and wear.
Uses Single or multi-coloured patchwork blanket, shawl, bath-mat, bedroom rug, linen bag or tabard.

Make 12ch and join into a ring with a ss into first ch.
Round 1 3ch, 1tr into ring * (yrh, insert hook into ring, yrh, draw lp through, yrh, draw through 2 lps) 6 times, yrh, draw through 6 lps, yrh, draw through rem 2 lps – called bobble – 4tr into ring, rep from * twice more, bobble, 2tr into ring, ss to 3rd of first 3ch.
Round 2 3ch, 1tr into same place, * 1tr into each of next 3 sts, 2tr into next tr, 1ch, 2tr into next tr, rep from * 3 times more, but omit the last 2tr and ss to 3rd of first 3ch.
Round 3 3ch, 1tr into same place, * (1tr into next tr, bobble into next tr) twice, 1tr into next tr, 2tr into next tr, 2ch, 2tr into next tr, rep from * 3 times more, but omit the last 2tr and ss to 3rd of first 3ch.
Round 4 3ch, 1tr into same place, * 1tr into each of next 7 sts, 2tr into next tr, 3ch, 2tr into next tr, rep from * 3 times more, but omit last 2tr and ss into 3rd of first 3ch.
Round 5 3ch, 1tr into same place, * 1tr into each of next 2tr, (bobble into next tr, 1tr into next tr) 3 times, 1tr into next tr, 2tr into next tr, 4ch, 2tr into next tr, rep from * 3 times more, but omit last 2tr and ss to 3rd of first 3ch.
Round 6 3ch, 1tr into same place * 1tr into each of next 11 sts, 2tr into next tr, 4ch, 2tr into next tr, rep from * 3 times more, but omit last 2tr and ss to 3rd of first 3ch.
Fasten off.

Flower square

Materials Medium-weight wool, silky yarn or crochet cotton for a deep sculptured effect.
Uses All-over repeat for cushion or lacy bedspread centre panel, hot water-bottle cover or padded teacosy.

Make 4ch and join into a ring with a ss into first ch.
Round 1 * 2ch, 4tr into ring, ss into ring, rep from * 3 times more.
Round 2 Ss into back of 3rd tr, * keeping yarn at back of work, 4ch, ss into back of 3rd tr of next gr, rep from * twice more, 4ch, join with a ss to first ss.
Round 3 Into each lp work 1ss, 5tr, 1ss.
Round 4 * 6ch, 1ss into back of ss between petals, rep from * 3 times more.
Round 5 3ch, (2tr, 3ch, 3tr) into same lp, * 1ch, (3tr, 3ch, 3tr) into next lp, rep from * twice more, 1ch, join with a ss to 3rd of first 3ch.
Round 6 3ch, (2tr, 3ch, 3tr) into same sp, * 1ch, 3tr into 1ch sp, 1ch, (3tr, 3ch, 3tr) into 3ch sp, rep from * twice more, 1ch, 3tr into 1ch sp, 1ch, join with a ss to 3rd of first 3ch.
Round 7 3ch, (2tr, 3ch, 3tr) into same sp, * (1ch, 3tr into 1ch sp) twice, 1ch, (3tr, 3ch, 3tr) into 3ch sp, rep from * twice more, (1ch, 3tr into 1ch sp) twice, 1ch, join with a ss to 3rd of first 3ch. Fasten off.

Dandelion

Materials Light-weight wool, slub linen or cotton yarn for an embossed effect.
Uses Appliqué motif (with embroidered stalks) for cardigan pocket or sweater front; straw hat-brim trim or lapel badge.

Make 4ch and join into a ring with a ss into first ch.
Round 1 1ch, 11dc into ring, ss to first ch.
Round 2 Working into front half only of each dc, work (1dc, 4ch, 1dc) into each dc.
Round 3 Working into back half only of each dc of rnd 1, * 6ch, (1dc, 6ch, 1dc) into next dc, rep from * to end.
Fasten off.

Relief Medallions

Greater depth is given to fine crochet motifs by working over one or more additional threads and then working double crochet over this foundation. Relief motifs may either be incorporated into a simple net background – as a border or as an all-over repeat – or applied individually as a fashion accessory.

Spray of leaves

Materials Fine crochet cotton, linen thread, silk or lurex for well-shaped motifs.
Uses Cardigan pocket or sweater motif, or combine with all-over lacy stitch for cushion, shawl or bedspread.

For first leaf make 16ch.
Row 1 1dc into 2nd ch from hook, 1dc into each of next 13ch, 3dc into next ch, cont along other side of foundation ch, 1dc into each of next 14ch, 1ch, turn.
Row 2 Working throughout into the back half only of each st, 1dc into each of next 11dc, 1ch, turn.
Row 3 1dc into each of next 11dc, 3dc into next st, 1dc into each of next 12dc, 1ch, turn.
Row 4 1dc into each of next 12dc, 3dc into next dc, 1dc into each of next 10dc, 1ch, turn.
Row 5 1dc into each of next 10dc, 3dc into next dc, 1dc into each of next 10dc, 1ch, turn.
Row 6 1dc into each of next 10dc, 3dc into next dc, 1dc into each of next 8dc, 1ch, turn.
Row 7 1dc into each of next 8dc, 3dc into next dc, 1dc into each of next 8dc, 1ch, turn.
Row 8 1dc into each of next 8dc, 3dc into next dc, 1dc into each of next 6dc.
Fasten off.
Make 2 more leaves in the same way.
For stalk, make 30ch, ss into base of one leaf, 8ch, ss into base of second leaf, turn; working over 3 strands of yarn work 1dc into each ch to end, turn, ss into each of first 30 sts, then ss to base of third leaf (this will now be opposite to the first leaf).
Fasten off.

Rose

Materials Very fine crochet cotton, silk or linen thread for forming tiny delicate flowers.
Uses Spot appliqué for party cardigan, pearl-centred buttons, wide hat-brim decoration on hanging ribbons, drawstring fob ends, haircomb or hairslide trim.

Wind the yarn 3 or 4 times round a finger, remove the loop from finger and fasten with a ss.
Round 1 1ch, 17dc into ring, ss to first ch.
Round 2 6ch, miss 2dc, 1htr into next dc, * 4ch, miss 2dc, 1htr into next dc, rep from * 3 times more, 4ch, ss into 2nd of first 4ch.
Round 3 Into each 4ch lp work (1dc, 1htr, 3tr, 1htr, 1dc), end with a ss into first dc.
Round 4 Ss into back of htr on rnd 2, * 5ch, keeping yarn at back of work 1ss into back of next htr on rnd 2, rep from * 4 times more, 5ch, ss into same htr as first ss.
Round 5 Into each 5ch lp work (1dc, 1htr, 5tr, 1htr, 1dc), end with a ss to first dc.
Round 6 Ss into back of ss on rnd 4, * 6ch, keeping yarn at back of work 1ss into next ss on rnd 4, rep from * to end.
Round 7 Into each 6ch lp work (1dc, 1htr, 7tr, 1htr, 1dc), end with a ss into first dc.
Fasten off.

Four leaf clover

Materials Fine wool, silky yarn, metallic thread or crochet cotton for a delicate look.
Uses Single motif for lapel accessory, draped party dress neck or jacket trim, or link with lacy pattern for bedcover.

Make 5ch and join into a ring with a ss into first ch.
Round 1 1ch, 13dc into ring, ss to first ch.
Round 2 1ch, 1dc into next dc, * 4ch, ** yrh twice, insert hook into next st, yrh, draw lp through, (yrh, draw through 2 lps) twice ** rep from ** to ** twice more into same st, yrh, draw through 4 lps on hook, 3ch, 1dc into each of next 2dc, rep from * 3 times more, make 6ch for stalk, turn and work 1ss into each ch, then 1ss into next dc on flower.
Fasten off.

Hibiscus

Materials Very fine cotton, rayon, silk or metallic thread for a detailed flower effect.
Uses Random appliqué pattern for sheer fabric dress or evening wrap, sash trim for dress bodice, mock buttons, or link with lacy pattern for shawl or throwover.

This medallion uses 2 colours, A and B.
Using A, make 6ch and join into a ring with a ss into first ch.
Round 1 3ch, 19tr into ring, ss to 3rd of 3ch. Break off A.
Round 2 Join in B, * 1ch, 1tr into next tr, 2tr into next tr, 1tr into next tr, 1ch, 1dc into next tr, rep from * 4 times more, but omit last dc and work a ss into same place as join.
Fasten off.
Cut a few strands of each colour and join to back of work to form stalk.

Shamrock

Materials Fine crochet cotton, silk or rayon for a raised effect.
Uses Appliqué motif for bride's veil, sweater or cushion; combine with lacy pattern for table linen border.

Make 16ch.
Round 1 1dc into first of the 16ch, to make 1 lp, (15ch, 1dc into same ch as before) twice. 3 lps now made.
Round 2 Lay a length of yarn along the work, then working over this thread, work 22dc into each 15ch lp, ss into first dc.
Round 3 Working over length of yarn, miss 1dc, * 1dc into each of next 20dc, miss 2dc (1dc of this lp and 1dc of next lp) rep from * twice, ss into first dc, 25ch, turn.
Stalk 1dc into 2nd ch from hook, then over length of yarn work 1dc into each ch, then work 1ss into first dc of shamrock.
Fasten off.

TUNISIAN CROCHET

Also known as Afghan stitch, this draws on the techniques of both knitting and crochet. A long hooked needle is used and the work differs from crochet in several ways; no turning chains are required and the rows are worked in pairs without turning the work (see p.13). Tunisian stitches generally produce a closely-woven fabric.

Tunisian stitch

Materials Medium-weight synthetic yarn or double knitting wool for a dense texture and warmth; crochet cotton, silk or rayon for a cool firm fabric.
Uses All-over pattern for father and son jerkin and matching cap; mother and daughter waistcoat front, shoulder bag or floor cushion inset panel.

Make a foundation row of 20ch.
Row 1 Working from R to L, miss first ch, insert hook into 2nd ch from hook, yrh and draw through 1 loop, * insert hook into next ch, yrh and draw through 1 loop, rep from * to end of ch length keeping all loops on hook.
Row 2 Working from L to R, yrh and draw through first 2 loops on hook, * yrh and draw through next 2 loops on hook, rep from * to end leaving 1 loop on hook.
Row 3 Working from R to L, miss first vertical loop on RS of fabric, * insert hook from R to L into next vertical loop, yrh and draw through 1 loop, rep from * to end keeping all loops on hook.
Row 4 Work as row 2.
Repeat rows 3 and 4 throughout.

Fan stitch

Materials Medium-weight yarn for a nubbly texture; baby wool for softness.
Uses Mother and daughter cardigan inset panel or all-over repeat for loose slipover; bedjacket, baby's dress or shawl border.

Make a no. of ch with a multiple of 3 sts plus 1 extra.
Work 3 rows in plain Tunisian stitch, (see p.87).
Row 4 Yrh and draw through first loop, * 2ch, yrh and draw through the loop on hook and the next 3 loops, rep from * to end.
Row 5 1ch, * insert hook into each of next 2ch and draw up a loop, insert hook into the vertical loops of the 3 sts which were worked tog and draw up a loop, rep from * to end, working into the last 2ch, then into the vertical loop of the end st.
Row 6 Work the sts off in pairs in the usual way.

Queen lace stitch

Materials 4-ply wool, acrylic or cotton yarn for a classic look; random-dyed yarn for a gently mottled effect.
Uses Dress bodice or all-over pattern for slipover, classic-style cardigan or hat; baby's coat, bonnet or cot blanket.

Make an even no. of ch and work first 2 rows in plain Tunisian stitch, (see p.87).
Row 3 * Lay yarn across front of work, insert hook from right to left in front of first 2 sts tog, yrh and draw lp through purlwise, insert hook between sts, yrh and draw lp through, rep from * to last st, insert hook into last st, yrh, draw lp through.
Row 4 As row 2.
Rep rows 3 and 4 throughout.

Colour squares

Materials Silk, rayon, cotton or crêpe yarn for a soft luxurious effect; double knitting, bouclé wool or tweedy mix for wintry days.
Uses All-over repeat for long evening jacket or long fringed silky scarf; man's sweater or waistcoat inset panel or all-over pattern for child's double-breasted jacket and matching cap.

This pattern uses 2 colours, A and B.
Make a no. of ch divisible by 8.
Row 1 Using A, insert hook into 2nd ch, yrh, draw lp through, (insert hook into next ch, yrh, draw lp through) twice; using B, (insert hook into next ch, yrh, draw lp through) 4 times, cont in this way working 4 lps in A and 4 lps in B.
Row 2 Using B, yrh, draw through one lp, (yrh, draw through 2 lps) 3 times, using A, (yrh, draw through 2 lps) 4 times, cont in this way to end.
Cont in this way, work 4 more rows, then alternate the colours and work 6 rows.
Rep these 12 rows throughout.

Brocade stitch

Materials Shetland, double knitting, crêpe wool or acrylic mix for warmth and wear.
Uses All-over pattern for ski sweater and matching hat, shoulder bag, slipper socks, blanket panel or travel rug.

This pattern uses 2 colours, A and B.
Using A, make a no. of ch divisible by 10, plus 2.
Work first 2 rows in plain Tunisian stitch, (see p.87).
Row 3 Using B, insert hook into first lp without drawing yarn through – called 1 sl st – * work 2 plain sts, (yrh, insert hook into next st, draw lp through, yrh, draw through 2 lps – called tr st –) 4 times, 2 plain sts, 2 sl sts, rep from * to end.
Row 4 Using B, as row 2.
Rows 5 and 6 Using A, as plain Tunisian stitch.
Row 7 Using B, 2 tr sts, * 2 plain sts, 2 sl sts, 2 plain sts, 4 tr sts, rep from * to end.
Row 8 Using B, as row 2.
Rep these 8 rows throughout.

Narcissus lace stitch

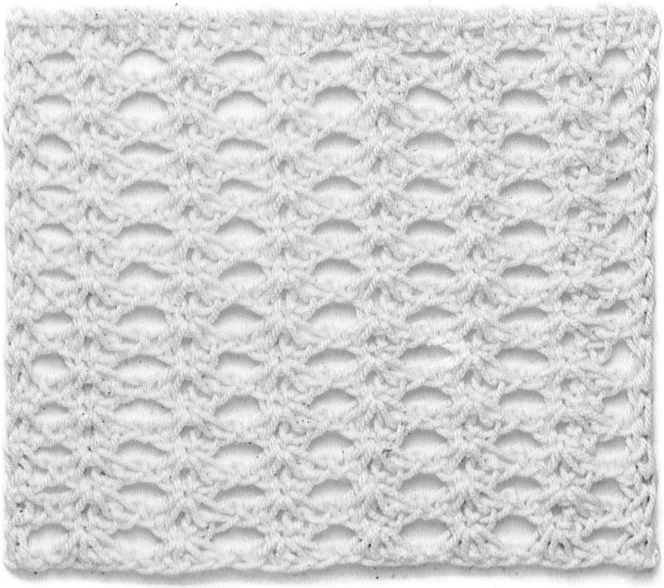

Materials Medium-weight wool, crêpe or synthetic yarn for a lacy look.
Uses Dress yoke or inset panel; all-over design for baggy T-shirt, bedjacket or shawl border.

Make a no. of ch divisible by 4, and work first row in plain Tunisian stitch, (see p.87).
Row 2 Yrh, draw through 2 lps, * 4ch, yrh, draw through 5 lps, rep from * until 3 lps rem on hook, 3ch, yrh, draw through 3 lps, 1ch.
Row 3 Insert hook into first ch, yrh, draw lp through, rep into each of next 2ch, * (insert hook into next ch, yrh and draw lp through) 4 times, rep from * to end.
Rep rows 2 and 3 throughout, ending with row 2.

Edgings

This group of stitch patterns offers one of the most versatile ranges of stitch decoration, texture and uses. Applied edgings need not be restricted to crocheted articles, but may be quite successfully applied to hand or machine knitting, or to woven fabric. All the stitch patterns illustrated may be used as edgings but can easily be made into double-edged trim by repeating the pattern in the opposite side of the foundation row. It is a good idea to wash cotton trim before applying to prevent any shrinking pulling the article out of shape.

Piranesi edging

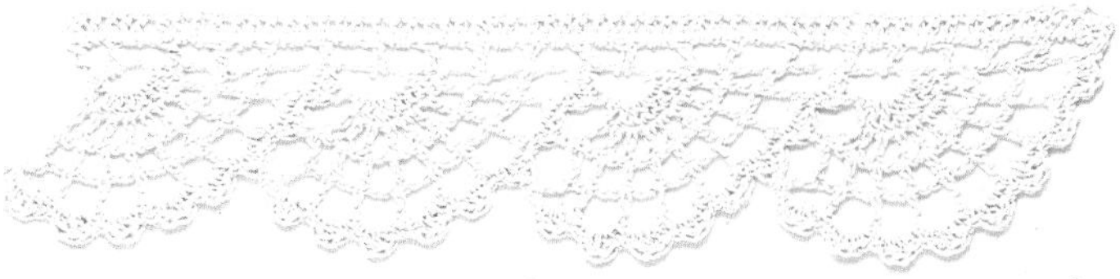

Materials Fine rayon or crochet cotton for a pretty look.
Uses Trim for print nightie and matching négligé, petticoat, lower edge of woven fabric overblouse or guest towel set.

Make 8ch and join into a ring with a ss into first ch.
Row 1 3ch, 8tr into ring, turn.
Row 2 4ch, 1tr into 2nd tr, * 1ch, 1tr into next tr, rep from * 5 times more, 1ch, 1tr into 3rd of 3ch.
Row 3 5ch, 1tr into 2nd tr, * 2ch, 1tr into next tr, rep from * 5 times more, 2ch, 1tr into 3rd of 4ch.
Row 4 6ch, 1tr into 2nd tr, * 3ch, 1tr into next tr, rep from * 5 times more, 3ch, 1tr into 3rd of 5ch.
Row 5 * (1dc, 3tr, 1dc) into 3ch sp, rep from * 7 times more, 8ch, turn and ss into 2nd of first 3tr, turn.
Row 6 3ch, 8tr into 8ch lp, turn.
Row 7 4ch, 1tr into 2nd tr, * 1ch, 1tr into next tr, rep from * 5 times more, 1ch, 1tr into 3rd of 3ch, ss into 2nd tr of next group of 3, turn.
Row 8 5ch, miss first tr, 1tr into next tr, work as row 3 from * to end.
Row 9 Work as row 4, then ss into 2nd tr of next group of 3, turn.
Rep rows 5 to 9 for the length reqd, then work row 5, omitting the 8ch at the end of row.

Heading

Working along straight edge of work, 5ch, 1tr into next row end, * 2ch, 1tr into next row end, rep from * to end, turn.
Next row 3ch, * 2tr into 2ch sp, 1tr into next tr, rep from * to end, working last tr into 3rd of 5ch.
Fasten off.

Picot arch edging

Materials Fine cotton or rayon yarn for household trim.
Uses Finish for bedlinen, bedside tablecover, net curtain or pretty kitchen shelf edging.

Make a ch the length reqd, having a no. of ch divisible by 3 plus 1, 2ch, turn.
Row 1 1tr into 4th ch from hook, 1tr into each ch to end.
Row 2 * 3ch, miss next 2tr, 1tr into next tr, rep from * to end.
Row 3 Ss into first lp, * 6ch, ss into 4th ch from hook, 2ch, 1dc into next lp, rep from * to end.
Fasten off.

Nugget edging

Materials Fine to medium-weight wool, cotton, lurex or synthetic yarn for a delicate finish.
Uses Sweater or bolero trim, silk scarf edging or straw hat band with added flowers.

Make a ch the length reqd, having a no. of ch divisible by 8 plus 3, 2ch, turn.
Row 1 1tr into 4th ch from hook, 1tr into each ch to end.
Row 2 3ch, 1tr into each of next 2tr, * (2ch, miss 2tr, 1tr into next tr) twice, 1tr into each of next 2tr, rep from * to end, working last tr into t-ch.
Row 3 4ch, leaving last lp of each on hook work 3dtr into next sp, yrh, draw through all 4 lps on hook, * 9ch, leaving last lp of each on hook work 3dtr into next sp, then 3dtr into next sp after the 3tr, yrh, draw through all 7 lps on hook, rep from * to end, ending with 9ch, work a 3dtr cluster into last sp, 1dtr into t-ch.
Row 4 Ss into top of first cluster, work (1dc, 1htr, 7tr, 1htr, 1dc) into each 9ch lp, ss into top of last cluster.
Fasten off.

Triangle edging

Materials Very fine cotton, linen or silk thread for the tiniest border trim.
Uses Finish for baby clothes, handkerchiefs and hems, greetings card or picture mount.

Make a ch the length reqd, having a no. of ch divisible by 4 plus 1, 2ch, turn.
Row 1 1tr into 4th ch from hook, 1tr into each ch to end.
Row 2 3ch, 3tr into first tr (edge st), * miss 3tr, 1dc into next tr, 3ch, 3tr into same tr, rep from * to end, ending with miss 3tr, 1dc into t-ch.
Fasten off.

Fan edging

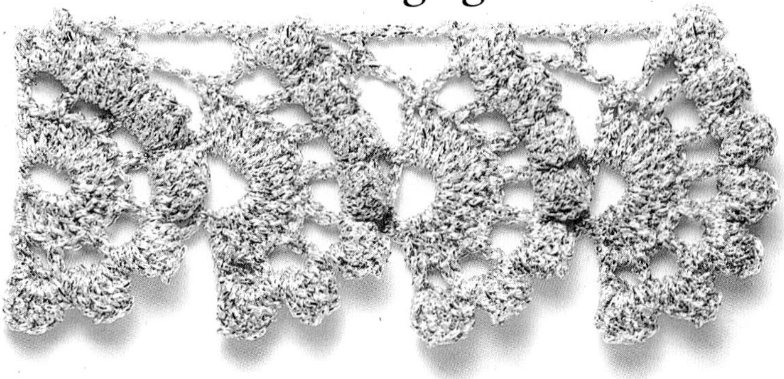

Materials Medium-weight crêpe, rayon, lurex or crochet cotton for a bold trim; fine cotton or silk for a delicate finish.
Uses Lower edges of slinky evening dress and jacket or curtain tieback; circular table cover or cushion trim.

Make 10ch and join into a ring with a ss into first ch.
Row 1 3ch, 14tr into ring, 5ch, turn.
Row 2 Miss first tr, (1tr into next tr, 2ch, miss 1tr) 6 times, 1tr into 3rd of 3ch, 3ch, turn.
Row 3 * 7 tr into next sp, take hook out of lp, insert it into 3rd of 3ch, then into the lp and draw lp through – called popcorn st – 3ch, rep from * 5 times more, 1 popcorn st into last sp, 10ch, turn.
Row 4 Miss first 2 sps, (1dc, 5ch, 1dc) into next sp, 3ch, turn.
Row 5 13tr into 5ch lp, 1dc into 10ch lp, 5ch, turn.
Row 6 Miss dc and first tr, (1tr into next tr, 2ch, miss 1tr) 6 times, 1tr into 3rd of 3ch, 3ch, turn.
Rep rows 3 to 6 for the length reqd, ending with a 3rd row. Do not turn or break off yarn.

Heading
1tr into sp below last popcorn st, * 5ch, 1tr into 10ch lp, 5ch, 1tr into sp below next popcorn st, rep from * to end.
Fasten off.

Scallop edging

Materials Plain or random-dyed rayon, silk or synthetic yarn for a firm, pretty edging.
Uses Edging for knitted or crocheted cardigan or bedjacket; pillow, petticoat or pram cover trim.

Worked into a row of dc on edge of work, having a multiple of 6dc plus 1.

1ss into first dc, * miss 2dc, 5tr into next dc, miss 2dc, 1ss into next dc, rep from * to end.

Richelieu edging

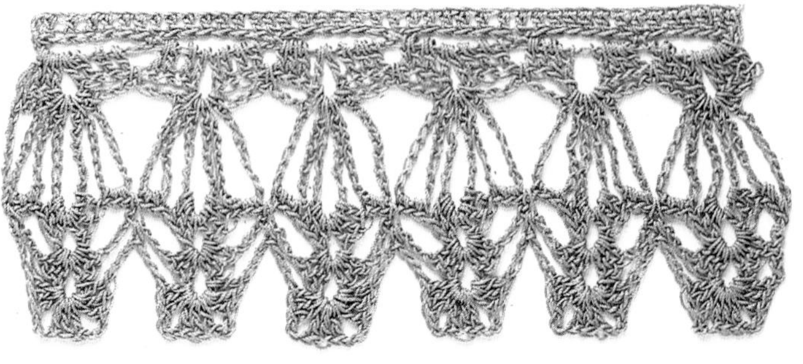

Materials Medium-weight rayon, lurex or cotton yarn for soft furnishing.
Uses Trim for lampshade, roller blind, cushion set or lower edge of upholstered furniture.

Make a ch the length reqd, having a number of ch divisible by 7 plus 1, 2ch, turn.
Row 1 1tr into 4th ch from hook, 1tr into each ch to end.
Row 2 * 6ch, miss 6tr, 1dc into next tr, rep from * to end.
Row 3 Ss into first lp, 3ch, (3tr, 2ch, 4tr) into same lp, * (4tr, 2ch, 4tr) into next lp, rep from * to end.
Row 4 * 3ch, 1dc into 2ch sp, (15ch, 1dc into same sp) 3 times, 3ch, 1dc between groups of tr, rep from * to end, working last dc into 3rd of 3ch at beg of row 3.
Row 5 8ch, * 3dc into first 15ch lp, (3tr, 2ch, 3tr) into next lp, 3dc into next lp, rep from * to end.
Row 6 * 3ch, (3tr, 2ch, 3tr) into 2ch sp, 3ch, 1dc bet groups of dc, rep from * to end, working last dc into 8th of 8ch.
Row 7 * 3ch, (3tr, 2ch, 3tr, 2ch, 3tr) into 2ch sp, 3ch, 1dc into dc, rep from * to end, omit last dc and end with a ss into first of 3ch. Fasten off.

Rose edging

Materials Fine crochet cotton, rayon or silky yarn for a light summery look.
Uses Light fabric dress neck and sleeve edge trim, lingerie or bedroom lampshade.

First motif
Make 8ch and join into a ring with a ss into first ch.
Round 1 1ch, 11dc into ring, ss to first ch.
Round 2 * 5ch, miss 1dc, 1dc into next dc, rep from * 4 times more, 5ch, 1dc into ss at end of rnd 1.
Round 3 Into each 5ch lp work 1dc, 1htr, 5tr, 1htr and 1dc.
Round 4 Keeping hook behind petals just worked, work 1dc into first dc on rnd 2, * 4ch, 1dc into 3rd ch from hook – called picot – 5ch, pc, 2ch, 1dc into dc on rnd 2 bet next 2 petals, rep from * all round, ending with 1ss into first dc.
Fasten off.
Second motif
Work as given for first motif until the 4 rnds have been completed, but do not break off yarn.
To join motifs, work in rows as follows:
Row 1 Ss along to centre of next pc lp, 1dc into same lp, 4ch, pc, 5ch, pc, 2ch – called picot loop – 1dc into centre of next pc lp, turn.
Row 2 1 pc lp, 1dc into centre of next pc lp, 1 pc lp, 1dc into dc at base of pc lp on previous row, turn.
Row 3 Ss to centre of next pc lp, 1dc into same lp, 1 pc lp, 1dc into centre of next pc lp, turn.
Row 4 4ch, pc, 1ch, ss into centre any lp on first motif, 3ch, pc, 2ch, 1dc into next pc lp on 2nd motif, 3ch, pc, 2ch, 1dc into dc at base of previous row.
Fasten off.
Make as many motifs as reqd, joining each as shown, leaving one pc lp free at each side of join.
Heading
With right side facing join yarn to pc lp at top of first motif, 1dc into same place as join, * (5ch, 1tr into next pc lp) 4 times, 5ch, 1dc into next pc lp, rep from * to end.
Fasten off.
Scalloped edge
With right side of other edge facing join yarn to loop before the top lp of first motif, 5ch, pc, 3ch, * into next lp (at top of motif) work (1dtr, 3ch, 1dc into top of dtr) 6 times, then 1dtr, 5ch, 1dc into pc lp at join of motifs, 1 pc lp, 1dc into next lp, 5ch, rep from * along edge, ending with dtr gr as before, 5ch, pc, 2ch, 1dc into next pc lp.
Fasten off.

Elm edging

Materials Medium-weight cotton or rayon for a leafy finish.
Uses Roller blind or towel trim; trolley cloth or table cover.

First leaf
Make 16ch.
Row 1 1dc into 2nd ch from hook and into each of next 13ch, 3dc into last ch, cont along the other side of ch, 1dc into each ch to end, 2dc into same ch as first dc, turn.
From here, work always into the back half only of each st.
Row 2 1dc into each of next 13dc, 1ch, turn.
Row 3 1dc into each dc, 3dc into centre dc of gr of 3dc, 1dc into each dc along other side to 1dc before next 3dc gr, 1ch, turn.
Row 4 1dc into each dc to 3rd dc from end, working 3dc into centre dc of 3dc gr, 1ch, turn.
Rows 5, 6 and 7 As row 4.
Row 8 1dc into each dc to centre of 3dc gr, ss into centre dc.
Fasten off.
Second leaf
Work as for first leaf until 7 rows have been completed, 1ch, turn.
Row 8 1ss into corresponding dc on first leaf, 1dc into each dc to centre of 3dc gr, ss into centre dc.
Fasten off.
Make as many leaves as reqd, joining each as shown.
Heading
Row 1 Join yarn to centre dc of first leaf, 1dc into same place, * 7ch, keeping the last lp of each on hook, work 1dtr into centre dc along side of this leaf, then 1dtr into centre dc along side of next leaf, yrh and draw through all 3 lps on hook – called a joint dtr – 7ch, 1dc into centre dc at top of this leaf, rep from * to end, 4ch, turn.
Row 2 * (miss 1ch, 1tr into next ch, 1ch) 3 times, miss 1ch, 1tr into top of joint tr, 1ch, (miss 1ch, 1tr into next ch, 1ch) 3 times, miss 1ch, 1tr into dc, rep from * to end.
Fasten off.

Bouquet edging

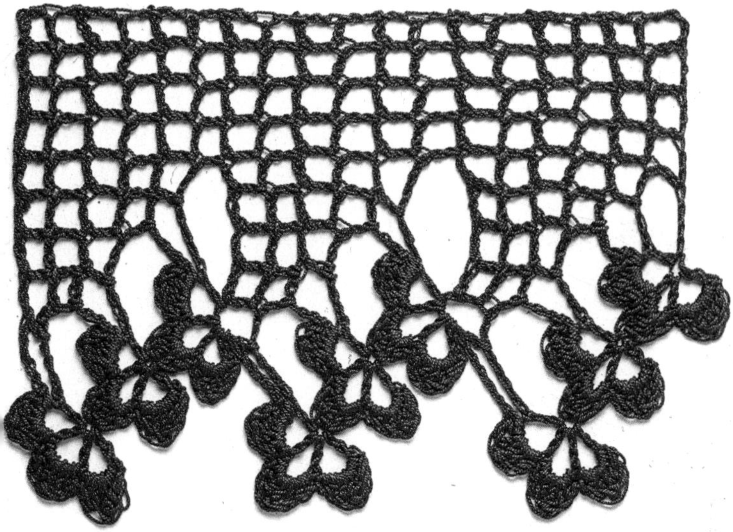

Materials Light-weight crochet cotton or random-dyed rayon for a deep lacy trim.
Uses Border for triangular shawl, filet-net café curtain or throwover bedspread.

Make 21ch.
Row 1 1tr into 8th ch from hook, (2ch, miss 2ch, 1tr into next ch) 3 times, 5ch, miss 3ch, (1tr, 3ch) 3 times into next ch, 1tr into same ch, 1ch, turn.
Row 2 (1dc, 1htr, 1tr, 1dtr, 1tr, 1htr, 1dc) into each of 3 3ch sps – shamrock made – 5ch, 1 tr into 5ch lp, (2ch, 1tr into next tr) 4 times, 2ch, miss 2ch, 1tr into next ch, 5ch, turn.
Row 3 Miss first tr, 1tr into next tr, (2ch, 1tr into next tr) 4 times, 2ch, 1tr into 5ch lp, 7ch, (1tr, 3ch) 3 times into dtr in centre of 2nd petal, 1tr into same place, 1ch, turn.
Row 4 Make a shamrock as before, 5ch, 1tr into 7ch lp, * 2ch, 1tr into next tr, rep from * to end, working last tr into 3rd of 5ch, 5ch, turn.
Row 5 As row 3 but working 2ch, 1tr into next tr) 6 times instead of 4 times.
Row 6 As row 4.
Row 7 Miss first tr, 1tr into next tr, (2ch, 1tr into next tr) 3 times, 7ch, miss 4 sps, (1tr, 3ch) 3 times into next sp, 1tr into same sp, 1ch, turn.
Rep rows 2 to 7 for length reqd, ending with a 6th row.
Fasten off.

Sunflower edging

Materials Fine rayon, synthetic yarn or crochet cotton for a pretty decorative finish.
Uses Roller blind or window pelmet trim, bedlinen or buffet runner border; curtain tie back.

First motif
Wind yarn about 10 times round one finger, then sl loop off finger.
Round 1 Work 40dc into ring, ss to first dc.
Round 2 1ch, 1dc into each dc to end, ss to first ch.
Round 3 As rnd 2.
Round 4 * 5ch, miss 1dc, 1dc into next dc, rep from * to end, working last dc into ss at end of rnd 3 (20 lps).
Round 5 Ss into first lp, 4ch, leaving last lp of each on hook, work 2dtr into same lp, yrh, draw through all 3 lps on hook, * 5ch, leaving the last lp of each on hook, work 3dtr into next lp, yrh, draw through all 4 lps on hook, rep from * to end, 5ch, ss to top of first cluster.
Fasten off.
Second motif
Work as for first motif until 4 rnds have been completed.
Round 5 Ss into first lp, 4ch, work a 2dtr cluster as on first motif, * 2ch, ss into a 5ch lp on first motif, 2ch, work a 3dtr cluster into next lp on 2nd motif, rep from * twice more, then complete as for first motif.
Make as many motifs as reqd, joining each in the same way.
Take care to leave 7 lps free at top and bottom of motifs between the 3 lps joining the motifs.
Heading
With right side facing join yarn to 7th lp before join on first motif, 9ch, 1dtr into next lp, * (4ch, 1dc into next lp) 3 times, 4ch, 1dtr into next lp, 4ch, leaving the last lp of each on hook work 1tr tr into next lp and 1tr tr into first free lp on next motif, yrh, draw through all 3 lps on hook, 4ch, 1dtr into next lp, rep from * to last motif, (4ch, 1dc into next lp) 3 times, 4ch, 1dtr into next lp, 4ch, 1tr tr into next lp, 7ch, turn.
Next row * 1tr into dtr, (4ch, 1tr into dc) 3 times, 4ch, 1tr into dtr, 4ch, 1tr into joined tr tr, 4ch, rep from * to end, working last tr into 5th of 9ch.
Fasten off.

Index

Acknowledgments

Contributors
Janet Swift

Assistants
Maggie Elliott
Gilly Squires

Artist
John Hutchinson

Photographers
Ian O'Leary
Steve Oliver

Typesetting
Contact Graphics Ltd

Reproduction
F. E. Burman Ltd